Earthbag Architecture

Building Your Dream with Bags

Hartworks LLC
1106 N. Swan St.
Silver City, NM 88061

Email: theoffice@hartworks.com

Websites: www.hartworks.com
www.greenhomebuilding.com
www.dreamgreenhomes.com
www.naturalbuildingblog.com

Table of Contents

Foreword

Ten years have elapsed since Kelly Hart and I decided to create EarthbagBuilding.com, and shortly thereafter Earthbag Building Blog (later renamed NaturalBuildingBlog.com). It's been a pleasure and honor working with Kelly. What started as a basic idea to spread the word about building with bags has grown by leaps and bounds as more people world-wide seek out lower cost, more sustainable building options. These two websites combined now average about 8,000 readers each day. The reasons for this growth are many. Escalating construction costs is the primary motivator for using alternative building methods such as earthbags. Factory made materials such as cement, steel and brick have become much more expensive and so many people simply cannot afford to build their own homes with these conventional materials.

Along with the rapid growth in popularity have come many innovations. The simplicity of natural building lends itself to creativity and experimentation, so builders often try new things. Being actively involved in every aspect of this movement means Kelly and I get to hear about countless innovations and share the best ideas with our readers.

Ten years ago the main earthbag options were building domes and other small, simple designs with subsoil and stabilized subsoil in polypropylene bags. There were very few earthbag building books, websites, workshops and trainers at that time. Kelly had been experimenting with scoria bag building, but few other main earthbag authors and builders have picked up on the idea, despite all the advantages of building with scoria -- lightweight, super insulating, easy to work with, faster, fire and pest resistant, etc.

The pace of earthbag innovation has greatly accelerated with a greater Web presence. This has made it much easier for people to discover the benefits of building with bags. It's no longer necessary to attend a workshop or buy a book; most building details are now clearly explained on our websites. Over the years our sites have documented all the best earthbag building projects, materials and methods. We've continuously added project profiles, house designs, images, videos, testing reports, articles and other related resources. We now have thousands of pages of free information.

Of all the changes from the last 10 years perhaps the most exciting have been improvements in building methods. These innovations can have a far reaching

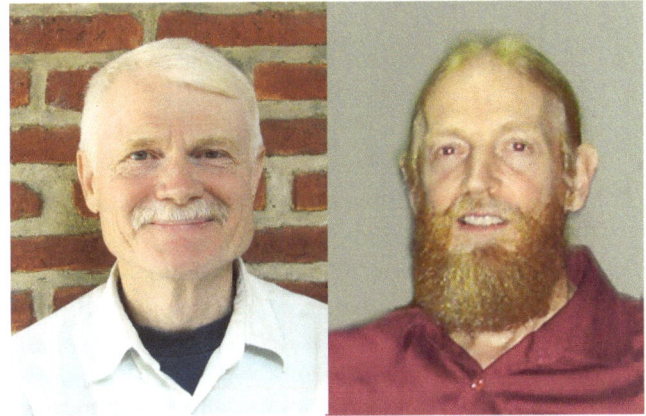

Kelly Hart   Owen Geiger

impact that effects how buildings are constructed for many years to come. Using lightweight scoria instead of heavier materials may make it possible for less muscular owner-builders to build their own home. This is but one of many such examples. Here's a sampling of earthbag innovations and developments over the last 10 years:

- **Greater use of lightweight, highly insulating materials** such as scoria, pumice, perlite and expanded clay granules and rice hulls;
- **Engineer Fernando Pacheco developed hyperadobe building** using raschel mesh tubing. Both Kelly and I are big fans of building with mesh bags and tubing, and have written extensively about this exciting development. The cost of the mesh material can be around one-quarter of the cost of poly bags, plus the mesh is ideal for binding with plaster;
- **Eternally Solar/Dr. Anderton's sand bag building method**;
- **Patti Stouter's hyperwattle method**;
- **Mechanized building to speed construction** has become more popular;
- **Many new fill materials** have been proposed and experimented with: foamed geopolymer, hempcrete, vetiver/lime, vetiver/clay, woodchip/clay, crushed limestone, lime or gypsum stabilized soil, caliche, mine tailings;
- **Confined earthbag with post and beam frame**;
- **Thin wall earthbag building** for speed and ease of construction;
- **Rainscreen to protect earthbag domes**;
- **Earthquake and hurricane resistant construction methods** such as pinning walls with rebar;
- **Low cost, alternative bond beams, lintels, foundations** and many other details;
- **Making uniform earthbags** using a wooden form as in Coron, Philippines;
- **Earthbag cool pantries, root cellars, water tanks, retaining walls, ponds**.

Owen Geiger, April, 2015

Introduction

In 1996 my wife Rosana and I were traveling around the Southwestern United States in a 40 foot bus I had converted into a traveling home and video production studio. I was collecting information and video footage for a documentary program called *A Sampler of Alternative Homes: Approaching Sustainable Architecture*. Somebody I talked to asked me, "Have you heard of earthbag building?" I hadn't, but I was determined to find out more about it, as it seemed like it should be covered in my program.

I soon discovered that an Iranian born architect named Nader Khalili was responsible for promoting the idea of making buildings by stacking bags, or tubes, filled with soil. He called this technique Superadobe. I arranged to meet him at his experimental compound, CalEarth (The California Institute of Earth Art and Architecture), in the California desert, to get a first hand introduction to the building technique. There I found an interesting collection of odd-shaped structures, mostly fashioned by stacking coils of large plastic tubing filled with soil. Khalili himself was a charismatic visionary with the zeal and drive to manifest his visions.

Around this time, I also visited a former student of Khalili's institute, who had built herself a small domed house and art studio using the Superadobe technique in Arizona, and footage of her explaining how she and her son had done it was used in the video program.

As we roamed around the American Southwest in our bus, we were always looking for beautiful places where we could park, and possibly develop landing pads for recurrent visits. One such spot turned up at a high alpine valley in Southern Colorado. The scenery was spectacular and the land was cheap, so we bought a small bit of acreage that actually had water, sewer, and electricity within easy range for hooking up.

The only hitch with just parking our bus there and enjoying life was that the property owners association that governed what could be done on the land had rules that expressly denied this. It would be possible to live in our bus while building a house, however, so we started to think about doing just that. My mind went back to the earthbag building I had seen, and I convinced Rosana that we could design and build an experimental home with earthbags, and do so quite cheaply.

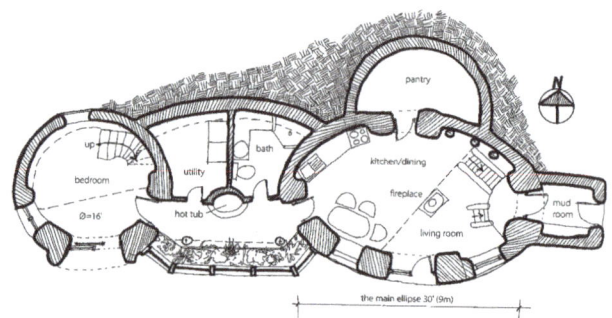

Fortunately, beyond the regulations applied by the homeowners association, the county had not adopted restrictive building codes. This made such experimental construction much more feasible. We designed a rather unusual looking plan that combined two domes with a central connecting space between them, and offered this to the committee that reviewed plans for the association. I was a little surprised that they accepted these plans without modification, so we were free to begin construction. I will describe the process of building this home in considerable detail later in the book.

Since completing that earthbag house (in about 2000), I have engaged in a number of other earthbag building projects, including a small dam for a pond, a large vault for a garage/shop/office complex, a small amphitheater project, a recessed pantry, and several independent small domes. I will describe all of this building as the story unfolds. I have learned a lot from all of this experience, that I will share with you.

While I was building the earthbag house, I continued to collect video footage of the process of the actual construction, which took nearly three years. I eventually produced another video program (since converted to DVD) titled *Building with Bags: How We Made Our Experimental Earthbag/Papercrete House*.

Around the time that I finished building the earthbag home I started writing a series of articles for our local newspaper in Colorado about sustainable architecture. At a certain point I thought about combining these articles into a single book, but then realized that a website devoted to the same topic might have more readers around the world. That is when www.greenhomebuilding.com was born and it continues to flourish to this day.

As an adjunct to this successful website, I founded www.dreamgreenhomes.com to combine the talents of several green architects and designers into a marketplace for stock green home plans.

One of these designers is Dr. Owen Geiger, who was a personal friend, and someone who was also bitten by the "earthbag bug." We talked about doing a book together about earthbag building, but then opted to launch another website instead: www.earthbagbuilding.com. Owen has gone on to write a guide to earthbag building as well as a how-to DVD on the topic.

In tandem with the earthbag building website, we

shared a blog on the same topic, that has now morphed into www.naturalbuildingblog.com. Owen does most of the blog posts for this, but I occasionally contribute as well.

All of these resources combined offer a wealth of information, not only about earthbag building, but about sustainable architecture in general. You can find most of the books and DVDs mentioned here available for purchase via the above mentioned websites.

You can anticipate reading more about the history of earthbag building in the next chapter. Then I will delve into the basics of what you need to know if you want to try your hand at building this way. After this I will describe in detail much of my direct experience with various projects. For years we have been publishing online information about the amazing variety of earthbag building that has been done around the world; now I will summarize some of this so you can understand how broad the scope of this revolutionary building technique is. Based on all of this, we can look at the basics of what is possible and suggest what the future of earthbag building might look like.

Hopefully, by the time you have finished reading this book you will have good idea of what can be done with earthbags, as well as have some understanding of the basics for doing it. Of course nothing can replace direct experience, so I encourage you to try your hand, starting with some small project, or participating with a workshop somewhere. Please bear in mind, however, that there are risks involved in any building. As you will read later, I have encountered many setbacks that I have had to overcome, and some of these could have resulted in injury. Neither I nor Hartworks, Inc. will have liability for loss, damage, or injury, resulting from the use of any information found in this book. I do hope that you enjoy the process of building as much as I have!

History of Earthbag Building

The idea of making walls by stacking bags of sand or earth has been around for over a century. Originally sandbags were used for flood control and military bunkers because they are easy to transport to where they need to be used, fast to assemble, inexpensive, and effective at their tasks of warding off both water and bullets. At first natural materials such as burlap were used to manufacture the bags; more recently woven polypropylene has become the preferred material because of its superior strength.

The use of sandbags has generally been associated with the construction of temporary structures or barriers. Using sandbags to build houses or permanent structures has been a relatively recent innovation.

In 1976 Gernot Minke at the Research Laboratory for Experimental Building at Kassel Polytechnic College in Germany began to investigate the question of how natural building materials like sand and gravel could be used for building houses without the necessity of using binders to consolidate the material. The use of fabric-packed bulk material was found to be a cost-efficient approach. They used pumice to pack in the bags, because it weighs less and has better thermal insulating properties than ordinary sand and gravel. Their first successful experiments were with corbelled dome shapes (an inverted catenary) which was obtained with the aid of a rotating vertical template mounted at the center of the structure.

In 1978, under Gernot Minke's direction, a prototype house using an earthquake-proof stacked-bag type of construction was built in Guatemala. They used cotton bags soaked in lime-wash to protect the material from rot and insects. When flattened, the bags measured roughly 3 X 4 inches (8 X 10 cm) Vertical bamboo poles placed on both sides of the bags and interconnected with wire loops gave the stacked bags stability. The bamboo rods were fixed to the foundation and to the horizontal tie beam at the top.

It was Iranian-born architect Nader Khalili who popularized the notion of building permanent structures with bags filled with earthen materials. Actually his first concept was to fill the bags with moon dust! Attending a 1984 NASA symposium for brainstorming ways to build shelters on the moon, Khalili coupled the old sandbag idea with the ancient adobe dome and arch construction methods from his homeland in the Middle East. He realized that bags filled with lunar "dirt" could be stacked into domes or vaults to provide shelter.

Khalili came up with a further refinement on this building concept on Earth: for a permanent, shock-resistant structure, why not place strands of barbed wire between the courses of bags, thus unifying the shell into a more monolithic structure?

At first Khalili was filling his experimental bags with desert sand, but then he evolved his idea of Superadobe, where bags or long tubes of polypropylene bag material would be filled with a moistened adobe soil, or cement-stabilized soil, that would dry into large adobe blocks. In this case the original bag material was merely the initial form and would not necessarily be an integral part of the eventual structure.

Soon after these first experiments, Khalili began publicizing his work through the media and conducting workshops on the techniques that he was perfecting. Many people who read about his work, visited his compound in Hesperia, California, or studied with him there, decided to go ahead with their own experiments with his ideas.

Among these "early adopters" were Joe Kennedy, Paulina Wojziekowska, Kaki Hunter and Doni Kiffmeyer, Akio Inoue, and myself. I believe that it was Joe Kennedy who coined the term "earthbag" to suggest that the bag could contain a variety of earthen materials.

Paulina Wojciechowska was the first to write an entire book on the topic of earthbag building: *Building with Earth: A Guide to Flexible-Form Earthbag Construction* was published in 2001. This featured some of her early experiments done at Khalili's CalEarth, along with several other case histories.

Akio Inoue, from Tenri University in Japan, has done extensive experimentation with earthbag construction, both on the campus of the University and in India and Africa. Above is pictured one of many projects that he has helped build for assistance programs.

Kaki Hunter and her husband Doni Kiffmeyer became enamored with earthbag construction after studying with Khalili, and worked on a variety of projects, both for themselves and for clients. In 2004 they wrote and got published another book, *Earthbag Building: the Tools, Tricks and Techniques* , based on their particular experience.

In the meantime, Nader Khalili was continuing the promotion of his Superadobe technique and eventually decided to patent the idea, which he obtained in the U. S. in 1999, using very general terms that cover using bags made of any material being filled with virtually any material, and combining these with barbed wired between the courses.

Many of us who had been engaged in promoting earthbag building on our own were contacted by Khalili and asked to enter into contracts with him in order to continue our work. It didn't take much research to discover that his patent could easily be disqualified because he had been publicizing his

techniques through various media for at least four years before he even applied for his patent. Patent law clearly states that such publicity occurring prior to one year before the patent application would disqualify it for consideration.

So now the door is wide open for anyone to take this concept and run with it, and more people are doing so all the time, all over the world. While Khalili and most of his students have focused primarily on using the bags to form large adobe blocks, others have tried filling them with a variety of other materials, such as crushed volcanic rock, crushed coral, non-adobe soils, gravel, and rice hulls.

Nader Khalili died in 2008, but his family continues to operate CalEarth where they conduct workshops and promote the Superadobe concept around the world. Earthbag building would certainly not be as popular today as it is without the dedication and work of this visionary.

Earthbag building is unique among all other building technologies in that it can be either insulation or thermal mass, depending on what the bags are filled with. Insulation will tend to isolate the interior space from the outside air, whereas thermal mass will slowly transfer that outside air temperature into the interior. This is a very important distinction, because these characteristics of a wall greatly influence how comfortable, economical, and ecological any given system will be.

Safety is of prime concern with all building technologies, and much experimentation and testing has been done to establish guidelines for many ways of building. Khalili established a relationship with the building department in Hesperia, California, where CalEarth is located, an area where earthquakes are naturally a great danger. In 1993 live-load tests to simulate seismic, snow and wind loads were performed on a number of domed earthbag structures at CalEarth and these exceeded code requirements by 200%.

In 1995 dynamic and static load tests were performed on several prototypes for a planned Hesperia Museum and Nature Center to be constructed using Khalili's Superadobe concepts with both dome and vault shapes. All of these tests exceeded ICBO and City of Hesperia requirements.

In 2006, at the request of Dr. Owen Geiger of the Geiger Research Institute of Sustainable Building, the Department of Civil and Mechanical Engineering of the U.S. Military Academy at West Point conducted several controlled and computer-monitored tests to determine the ability of polypropylene earthbags filled with sand, local soil, and rubble to withstand vertical loads. Their written report concluded that "overall, the earthbags show promise as a low cost building alternative. Very cheap, and easy to construct, they have proven durable under loads that will be seen in a single story residential home. More testing should prove the reliability and usefulness of earthbags."

Despite the success of these tests, earthbag building concepts have yet to be incorporated into the International Residential Building Code. Obviously more widespread acceptance of the demonstrated viability of earthbag building needs to occur!

It is difficult to know how many residences and other earthbag structures have been built at this point, certainly hundreds if not thousands. Many of us have been promoting the technique for use as emergency shelters, and some have been built for this reason. It is easy for folks to accept this way of building temporary shelters because it fits the historical model of sandbag use.

But many of us have also built substantial homes using earthbags, and in the process we've realized how truly versatile and sustainable the technique is. I wouldn't be surprised if many of these earthbag homes are still standing long after their conventional counterparts built contemporaneously have disintegrated.

Why Build with Earthbags?

Versatility is the first word that comes to mind when I consider the question, "Why build with earthbags?" I can't think of any other building technology, traditional or alternative, that offers so much versatility in terms of both building style and material behavior.

Earthbags are useful for making both straight and curved vertical walls, or they can be stacked to create various dome shapes, and these can be combined into some very interesting volumes, as pictured above.

Earthbags can be employed both below and above ground, since the polypropylene bag material commonly used is impervious to moisture damage. A variety of fill material can be used, depending on the need for insulation or thermal mass in the wall, and whether it needs to be resistant to moisture damage or not.

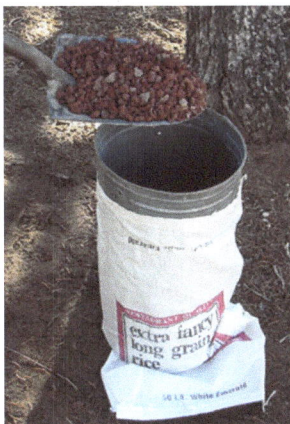

Another good reason to consider earthbags is that the construction can be extremely ecological. The foundation, walls, and even the roof (in the case of a dome) can be fashioned without the use of industrial materials (other than the bags themselves and some barbed wire) or even wood, which often is not sustainably harvested.

Earthbag building can be done quite economically; the bulk of the materials needed might be sourced for free on site, and the need for lots of concrete for a foundation could be eliminated. Of course, all of the usual supplies needed by any house, such as electrical and plumbing, will add to the expense.

Most of the process of building with earthbags is simple and requires very little experience or training. Owner/builders can take on an earthbag project with just a modicum of guidance, much of which can be found for free on the internet. We usually recommend starting with a small, non-critical project to gain some initial experience. While earthbag building is definitely hard work, it doesn't have to be back-breaking; it is possible to fill the bags in place, using buckets to carry the fill material, or lightweight fill materials can be used.

Durability is another factor in choosing earthbags; if properly detailed, with care in protecting the bag material both during the construction and with a good plaster, an earthbag building could last a very long time. In general, there is nothing that will rot. And at the end of the lifetime of such a building, most of the material can simply reunite with the earth.

The Basics

What Kind of Bags Work?

Burlap sacks were the most common choice for military and flood control sandbag projects in the early days. These worked well as long as the bags didn't rot from being exposed to too much moisture or sunlight over time, which was fine because they were considered temporary structures.

By far, the most common bag material in use today is polypropylene. This synthetic is stronger than burlap and resistant to damage from chemical or moisture exposure. It is quite vulnerable to damage from ultraviolet exposure from sunlight, however, so it must be protected from this as much as possible. One can buy polypropylene bags that have been given a UV resistant coating, but this only adds a few weeks of protection if the bags are left in the sunlight.

If you are going to fill the bags with loose material, it is pretty much imperative to use the poly bags, because they are stronger and will not deteriorate once they are plastered. If you intend to fill the bags with an adobe or stabilized material, then burlap or other natural materials for the bags may work, because once the wall has set up, the strength of the bag is not as important.

The fabric of the polypropylene bags is actually woven from small ribbons of the material. This is good, because it renders the bags breathable to some extent, meaning that any moisture added to the fill material can eventually dissipate, and the fill can form a solid block. For this reason, other, non-breathable, synthetic bags may not work well for earthbag building.

Polypropylene bags are commonly used for the storage of grains or animal feeds. This means that they can often be found as surplus or recycled bags. They can also sometimes be purchased as misprints from the bag manufacturers or wholesalers. Of course, it is also possible to buy quantities of new bags at reasonable prices, both online and from local outlets. See the Resources chapter for more information about this.

The best size for most earthbag projects would be bags that might be designated as 50 pound feed bags. These measure around 18 inches wide when flat and 32 inches long. This size works well, but the exact size is not critical; the bags could be somewhat larger or smaller, though I wouldn't go much smaller or the stability of the wall might be compromised. The wall will be about 18 inches thick when plastered. If you have larger bags, they might be used at the base, and if you have smaller bags, they might work near the top of a wall or dome. Larger bags would be more stable, but they take more material to fill them and they make thicker walls.

Then there is the question of whether to buy gusseted bags or not. Gussets, or pleats sewn into the bottom of the bag, keep the profile of the bag uniformly in one plane once they are filled and tamped into place. Without the gussets, there is a tendency for the pointed corners at the bottom to stick out, making the later plastering more difficult. Some people like to carefully fold and pin the bottom of the bag to avoid this, but I prefer to simply pound the points in with a hammer before plastering. Another trick is to turn the bag inside out to avoid the points.

Nader Khalili pioneered the use of long tubular sections of the same polypropylene material used to fabricate individual bags for layering on a wall. These tubes can be cut as long as needed to complete a particular wall section, slid onto a rigid filling tube or funnel, and then filled in place. It takes several people to accomplish this efficiently, but the result can be very aesthetically satisfying, strong, and quickly done.

The tubing material can be purchased (usually directly from a factory) as huge rolls, up to 6000 feet long. For some reason, there generally is no advantage economically in buying the large rolls over purchasing the individual bags, despite the obvious increase of manufacturing time and materials that goes into making the bags.

A recent innovation with bag material is the use of open mesh bags of the sort that is commonly used to package fruit. This mesh can also be purchased in

long rolls and used in a similar manner to the tubes of polypropylene. This technique was introduced by Fernando Pacheco, a Brazilian engineer, and he calls it "Hyperadobe." The mesh bags are often a raschel weave and the fiber is either polypropylene or other synthetics.

Hyperadobe takes Superadobe to a whole new level with many distinct advantages. The net bagging is generally cheaper than the woven poly material; the fill will dry out and cure faster; there may be no need for barbed wire in vertical wall designs; it creates a more monolithic structure due to direct bonding between courses; it is easier to gather the tubing on a canister for filling; there is better adhesion of plaster; the mesh provides an automatic plaster mesh reinforcement. The only disadvantage that I can think of is that it wouldn't work with some loose fill materials because of spillage.

Fill Material

The most common thermal mass fill material is a mix of sand and clay that approaches that used in other earthen wall systems, such as adobe, cob and rammed earth, where about 30% clay and 70% sand mix is ideal. But since the soil is encased in a strong bag, the exact formulation for this soil mix can have much more variability when used for earthbags. The objective is to have fill that does not shift around once it is moistened, tamped into place, and dried. Virtually any soil can be used in earthbags, but it is best to avoid heavy clay soils or fine, slippery sand. As long as you remove most of the larger rocks and organic debris, you should be fine. This means that it is often possible to use the earth beneath your feet at the site of building. What could be more sustainable than this?

How the bags will be used in a wall may determine what the best fill material is. Vertical walls are generally more forgiving than domes, which really need to be built with solid blocks of material. A dome created with shape-shifting fill could become unstable and collapse, unless it has proper reinforcing.

Another determining factor for choice of fill material is exposure to possible moisture issues, like underground situations or domes built in wet climates.

If there is not enough clay to bind the soil, it is possible to stabilize it with either Portland cement or

13

builder's lime. About 10% of these stabilizers could be enough, but it is best to run some tests with your soil to determine this. With domes, especially in climates where excess moisture could be an issue, it is advisable to stabilize the soil with cement to assure that the fill will never become soft enough to deform. We advise folks to avoid making domes in rainy climates, or at least to provide an additional, separate roof over the dome to shed water away from it.

Other, more insulating fill materials that have been used successfully include pumice and scoria (which are both lightweight volcanic stone), perlite, and even rice hulls. One could even experiment with recycling Styrofoam (EPS foam) or crushed plastic bottles as fill also. Of course, you would have to take into account the possible compressibility of these materials when designing the wall.

A special case for appropriate fill material is at the foundation or first course or two at the base of a wall. Here you want the wall to absolutely not deteriorate in moist conditions, nor do you want the wall to wick moisture upward into the rest of the wall. So we generally advise folks to fill the bags at this level with loose gravel. And because it is essential that such loose material never escapes, we advise the use of two bags (one placed inside the other) for double assurance it will be secure. A good stabilized plaster is essential to protect these bags.

Foundations

Earthbags themselves make good foundations, and have been used that way for many other building systems, such as for strawbale, cordwood, cob, etc. In this case, the bags are built up to the proper height for a stem wall that keeps the rest of the wall at least a foot above grade, well above snow level or possible back splash from rain hitting the ground.

All foundation systems must take into account the possibility of the underlying soil heaving with freezing weather or from expanding with moisture, as do heavy, expanding clays. The common way to avoid these problems is to dig down to a level that is below the frost depth for that region, or below any layers of heavy clay soil.

Prescriptive building codes often require continuous concrete foundations that comply with specific conditions and measurements. Such a foundation can be

used with earthbag construction, as long as the top of the concrete foundation is wide enough to accommodate the full width of the earthbags when compacted on top. In this case it would likely be a good idea to place a moisture barrier on top of the foundation wall, or start with a course of gravel-filled bags, to avoid the concrete from wicking moisture into the wall above.

Better than using a massive reinforced concrete foundation would be to employ a simple rubble trench foundation. These foundations were embraced by the famous architect, Frank Lloyd Wright. The idea is to dig a trench, at least as wide as the bags and plaster, down deep enough to get below the frost level. This trench is then filled with cobble stones, possibly graded so that the smaller aggregate is toward the top of the trench. This keeps the foundation stable from soil heaving and provides lots of spaces between the stones for moisture to accumulate and eventually drain. As seen in the above photo, the top of the rubble trench can be recessed some below grade, with the first course of gravel-filled bags placed so that they will provide a "toe" into the soil.

If the soil surrounding the trench does not drain well enough, then what is know as a French drain can be installed. This is a 3 - 4 inch drain pipe (usually plastic these days) that has been perforated so that water can seep into it from above and the sides. The pipe is laid toward the bottom of the trench and inclined slightly so that water will run to either a "daylight" location on the property or to an underground sump or drain field. This will allow any excess water to flow away from the foundation.

In the above photo the rubble trench is fairly shallow and no French drain is provided because the soil is pure sand that drains exceedingly well, making upheaval highly unlikely. The wire mesh visible in the photo was an attempt to keep the cobbles contained from migrating into the sand, and would not be needed in most applications.

There is no specific need to place a concrete cap on top of a rubble trench, but this could be done if the code requires it, or if the cobble stones used in the trench are fairly large and don't provide a good enough surface to lay the first course of bags on.

Additionally, the soil surrounding the base of the foundation wall should be graded so that it slopes away from the structure, keeping surface water from collecting near the foundation.

Another ecological foundation for earthbags could be carefully mortared stones built up on the rubble trench. This could be done for aesthetic reasons, or as a way to keep from needing to use gravel-filled bags. As with a concrete foundation, it would be prudent to place a moisture barrier between the mortared stones and the first course of bags.

Filling and Laying the Bags

Various simple ways have been used to make it easier to fill the bags. One common way is to cut the bottom out of a 5 gallon plastic bucket and use the top part as a funnel that holds the bag open. We have used a slightly tapered metal cylinder that is part of a commercial chicken feeder for the same purpose. I have seen stands made of metal that will hold an entire bag up and allow the fill to be shoveled in. No matter how you do it, it helps to have a way of keeping the top of the bag open while filling it. With the long continuous tubing material, it is essential to have some kind of

a chute to collect the loose fabric on that allows the fill to be placed toward the end, and then more tubing can be released from the chute as needed.

Unless you are working with lightweight fill material, I would advise you to fill the bags in place on the wall being built. This way you just need to carry smaller buckets or shovel fulls of material and save your back. A full bag of soil can easily weigh over 100 pounds, making the job of carrying or lifting it arduous.

Since the bottom of the bag has been sewn closed, it is best to place the bottom toward any opening in the wall to assure that nothing will tend to spill out. The simplest way to close the top of the bag is to just leave enough space at the top to be able to fold the bag over so that it will be compressed against the previously laid bag; usually about 8 to 10 inches is sufficient to do this. This does waste some potential length of the bag for filling, so you might prefer to physically close the bag at the top. If that seam will be pushed up against another bag, a simple way to close it is to turn the hem over once or twice and fasten it with nails, wire or common staples.

Using the full length of the bag has the advantage that the longer bags will have more space to overlap each other when laid in the preferred running bond pattern that is typical in laying brick walls. This makes for a more stable wall, and of course ultimately uses fewer bags to construct the wall.

In some circumstances, both ends of the bag might

be exposed and need to be securely closed. I have done this by actually hemming the top and sewing it with heavy thread, using very wide stitches. Another method that may be faster, is to use some metal wire that is stiff enough to simply jab it through the hemmed seam in several places and fold over the end of the wire to secure it.

Before closing the bag the fill at the top can be tapered so that it will conform to any angle formed by the arc of a small diameter circle to make a closer fit between two adjacent bags. Also it helps to push a bit on both sides of the bag at the top so that it is easier to fold or fasten the bag material. This all becomes second nature once you get into the swing of the work pattern.

When filling a bag in place on the wall, I usually place the bottom of the bag about where it will eventually be, so that once it is full and secured at the top, it can be simply pushed over to align it with the previously laid bag. This way there is no need to lift that heavy bag at all. A bit of pushing with your hands or feet will snug the bags into place so they can be tamped later.

Tamping the Bags

To consolidate the fill material and flatten the bags in place they need to be tamped soon after being laid. I usually wait until I have laid several, or even a whole course of bags, before doing this, since once you are up there tamping it is easier to do a whole section at once.

Stomping on the bags with your feet can do some tamping, but it is much more efficient and thorough to use a special tamping device. These can be purchased in some hardware stores, or fabricated in various ways.

My favorite tamper is home made, with a metal pipe handle welded to a scrap piece of heavy steel. The weight of this tool is an advantage, because it adds to the downward tamping thrust, so it doesn't take as much muscle to do the tamping; it is a bit heavier to lift, but I find it takes less effort than always putting more force into the downward thrust. The tamping blade is about as wide a standard bag, so each tamping action will do maybe 25% of the bag. The commercial tampers usually aren't as wide so they need to be moved around more to do the job.

Another approach to making your own tamper is to embed a long handle in a large can of wet cement and let it cure, creating a heavy circular tamper. I have never used one of these, but I think they may not do as good a job because they tend to make small circular indentations that would not be as uniformly flat, and definitely would take more tamping per bag to do a good job.

Some people like to also tamp the sides of a bag to make the wall flatter, which takes less plaster to cover. I haven't done this because I kind of like the deeper crevices between the bags to help key in the plaster. It is partly an aesthetic thing, depending on whether you like smoother walls or don't mind some uneven variation in the surface of a wall.

Barbed Wire

In most circumstances it is best to place barbed wire between each course of earthbags, ideally two strands of 4-pronged barbed wire placed parallel to each other. There are several reasons for doing this. First of all, the barbs on the wire tend to catch into the fabric of the bags, essentially stitching the two together into a more monolithic structure. The other main reason is that the wire provides tensile strength that the bag wall would lack without. This is especially important with dome structures, because they exert strong outward pressure on the bags from the weight of the bags above pressing downward and outward.

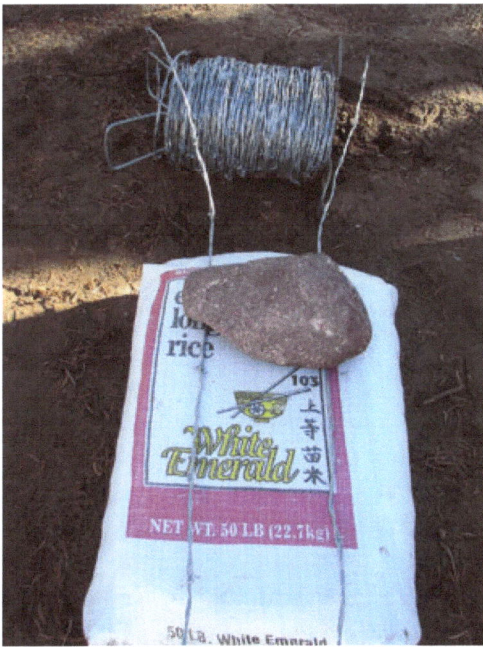

In general, the barbed wire holds everything together into a uniform matrix that resists the component bags from dislodging.

Barbed wire is nasty stuff to work with. It has a mind of its own and can gouge your hands easily. I always use heavy leather gloves when working with it and give it lots of respect. It helps to unwind enough wire from the spool to fit the desired place in advance, and then carefully bend it into a more or less straight line before placing it on the wall. Then, as shown in the photo, you can use stones, bricks, or other heavy objects to keep it where it should be on the course of bags. This should be done for the entire section of wall before going on to lay more bags on top of it.

To make it easier to position each bag perfectly into place, a metal "slider" can be very handy. This is a piece of sheet metal cut to approximately the size of a bag, with a 90 degree grip handle bent on one end. The idea is to put this slider over the barbed wire in the area where you want the next bag to be placed. Then, once the bag has been filled and laid down into its intended location, you can hold the bag in place with one hand and yank on the metal slider to remove it and allow the bag to drop into place. That is the theory, and it usually works pretty well. Otherwise, the bag will inevitably fall a little off from where it needs to be and then be stuck on the barbed wire and impossible to move without picking it up, which is a real nuisance.

The times I have dispensed with placing barbed wire between the bags is when I believe that the laws of gravity will prevail and keep a wall from pulling apart. An example of this is with an underground pantry that I made with outwardly inclined walls below grade. I figured that gravity was going to keep those walls inclined no matter what. Another example is with a small underground dome where the inward pressure of the surrounding soil would counteract the outward pressure of the dome itself, and the whole thing would be kept together by compression.

Protect the Walls

I have mentioned that polypropylene will degrade when exposed to the ultraviolet in sunlight, even with UV resistant bags. For this reason it is of paramount importance that the bags be protected from this hazard as much as possible. I can't stress this enough; I have answered countless emails from folks who discovered that their bag walls were disintegrating because they left them exposed too long. It only takes a few weeks for this to start to happen, and after awhile you can literally poke your finger through the material.

At times I have stretched tarps over projects and tied them to provide shade during the day. This can be quite effective, but difficult to keep in place when a stiff wind comes up and wants to sail the thing away. A somewhat more secure approach is to place the tarps directly over the wall and place weights to hold them into place. This way you can remove the tarp from just the section of wall that you are working on and then replace it when you are finished.

At times I have started to apply an initial plaster on the wall even before it is finished, just to help keep the sun away from that vulnerable material.

I have heard of folks using old paint to give a temporary protective coating to their earthbags once the wall has been erected, and I'm sure that this helps.

Once the wall is totally covered and cannot be seen by the sun, the bags should last for a very long time. Nobody really knows how long they will last because the synthetic material has not been in existence long enough to find out. Tests have shown that polypropylene is not degraded by water or most chemicals. I have gone back to interior walls that were left unplastered for nearly two decades, and they seem as strong, pliable and bright as the day I put them there. And once I dug down to check some earthbags that had been used as part of a dam for a pond and were

protected by heavy plastic and stones; although some tree roots had managed to infiltrate some of the bags, the poly material itself was as supple as ever.

What Shapes are Possible?

Earthbag building is quite versatile but there are some inherent limits to what is reasonably attempted. Vertical walls, whether curved or straight are always possible, although straight ones may require buttressing (discussed later). Curved vertical walls tend to be more stable because they are self-buttressing.

The potential height of vertical walls is governed by the same ratio that applies to other earthen wall systems. Wall height : thickness at the base is at least 10 : 1, so an earthbag wall that is 15 inches wide at the base should be no taller than 150 inches, which is 12.5 feet. If you want to go higher than that you need to use wider bags, at least at the bottom of the wall.

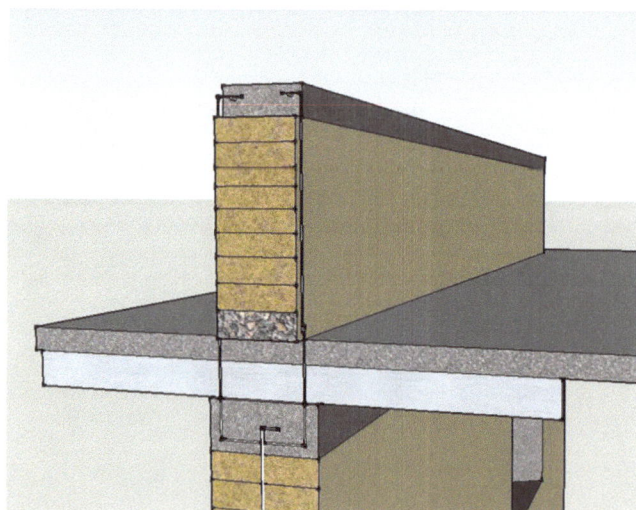

What about two story buildings that have vertical walls? It is possible, but they would have to be very carefully engineered. Above is pictured one concept for a two story building that was suggested by an engineer and might pass code in some places. You can see how the first story is wider than the second, and how steel anchors wrap the entire second story wall and are embedded in concrete bond beams at the top of each story's wall. In general, it is best to stick to one floor for most vertical walled earthbag buildings.

Domes are commonly built with earthbags, both simple isolated domes and complex interconnected ones. There is a limit to how large a diameter could be without compromising the integrity of the dome; this limit seems to be around 6 to 7 yards or meters. It is best to stay with circular dome patterns; I did make a large elliptical dome once, but had a lot of trouble keeping it stable, as you will read later.

Hemispherical domes are only possible with some extra supporting structure to help keep that shape. I once designed one with a wooden geodesic substructure that worked pretty well.

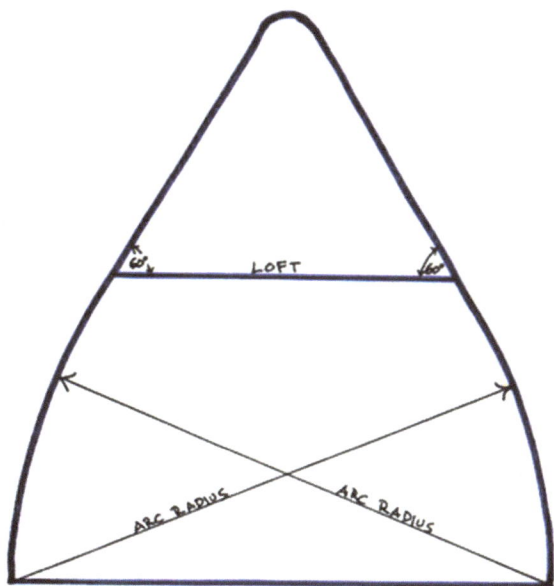

A better shape for a self-supporting dome is a catenary arch, or something that resembles this. A catenary arch is often described as the shape that a suspended

chain takes when the two ends are held out at the same level; if this shape is then inverted you have the shape of a catenary dome. The diagram shows one way to approach this shape that I have successfully built several times.

There is a common misconception that an earthbag vault, or tunnel with an inverted U-shape, would be easy to make and quite stable. In reality this is a shape that should be avoided, except in very small widths (perhaps no larger than 6 feet wide). The reason for this is that without massive buttressing, the outward pressure of the bags on the upper part of the vault on the lower portion can easily distort the shape enough for the top to collapse, posing a considerable hazard. Nader Khalili did make some vaulted structure using earthbags as vertical stem walls on the sides, but the vaulted portion was actually made with ferrocement.

I once built a large vaulted structure that was lined with earthbags, but the basic structure underneath was a commercial steel Quonset building. I will describe how I did this later in the book.

Buttressing

Certain types of walls are not sufficiently stable on their own and require some help staying vertical. The common way to stabilize them is with some form of periodic buttressing. A buttress is basically a short segment of wall that is attached to a longer wall, usually at a 90 degree angle, which keeps the major wall from any tendency to topple over sideways. The buttress needs to be integrally connected to the wall it supports so that the two can't separate. A well designed buttress can work either inside or outside of the wall it supports; this means that interior partition walls can also act as buttresses.

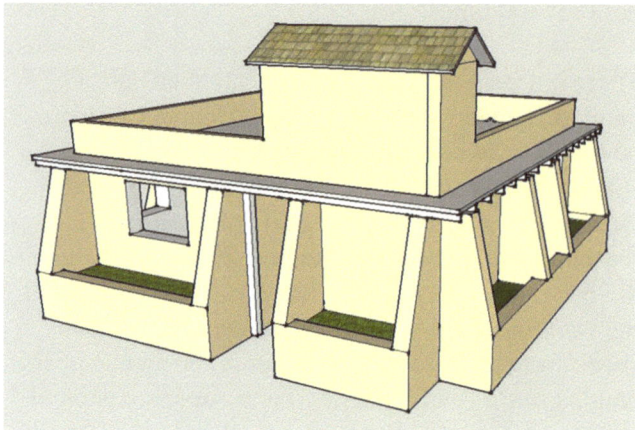

It is usually long straight walls that need buttressing because they can easily topple if they aren't. With earthbags, we usually advise that any straight wall longer than about 10 feet could benefit from being buttressed. In the above plan the exterior planter boxes are partially enclosed with tapered buttresses.

It is not uncommon to see plans that have buttresses at the corners, like the one above. I think this is partly stylistic and partly because it was found that with adobe buildings, the corners were vulnerable to earthquake damage and buttresses of this sort helped remedy that. With earthbags, the corners can be reinforced with the barbed wire that actually turns the corners, and with vertical steel rebar stakes driven down into the corner from the top of the wall. For this reason I think that corner buttressing is unnecessarily redundant.

It can be advantageous for buttresses to be placed

near wall openings, like doors and windows, to help stabilize them. The buttresses only have to extend a few feet outward from an exterior wall to be effective. And they don't really need to go all the way to the top; perhaps 2/3 of the way up the wall is sufficient. These buttresses can taper as they go up; in fact they can provide a decorative style, like those pictured with the stepped buttress on the circular structure.

In general, circular or curved walls are inherently stable enough not to require buttressing. This is why wandering or serpentine fence walls are so strong; they just don't want to tip over, even with lateral pressure. Round houses can envelop a very large space without any interior partitions or external buttresses for this reason.

Domes may require an interior buttress at the doorway that allows a vertical door to be installed. Either this, or an external vault or roofed area needs to be arranged to make it possible to install the vertical door. The above photo shows two different styles of creating such an interior buttress.

Openings

Doors and windows provide challenges for the integrity of an earthbag wall. Any opening creates a place where the matrix of the wall is torn, so to speak, and the edges of the opening need to be stiffened. There are various ways to accomplish this stiffening.

Doors can be made rigid by creating a metal or wooden frame around them that is integrally connected to the earthbag wall. This "door buck" can then be used for attachment of the door itself. One good way to connect the door buck to the bags is to provide

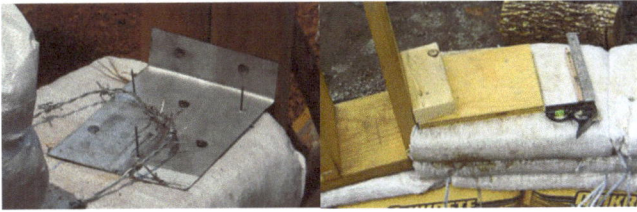

periodic anchor plates within the wall as it is being erected. These can be plywood or metal plates that either have a piece of solid wood attached at one end or have the metal edge turned 90 degrees. A bunch of nails can be driven through them in both directions that get embedded into the bags placed below and above them. The solid wood or metal edge is exposed at the doorway in the same plane as the door buck to which it can be attached. Window bucks can be created and attached in the same manner as door bucks.

A simple door or window buck may not be sufficiently strong on the top of the frame to support the weight of the wall or roof that may be above it. It is important to make sure that an adequate "header" be provided to support such weight, and this could be a larger beam of wood that is wide enough to support the bags. In some cases, when the top of the door or window is quite close to the top of the wall where there would normally be a reinforced "bond beam" (discussed later), then this beam itself will act as a sufficient header. Another way to deal with the weight of the wall above a door or window is to make an arched opening there.

Windows can be created in shapes other than rectangular, such as circular or triangular. In this case it

is possible to insert an appropriate frame for these shapes as the wall is being built, with the bags jammed up against them. I have done this with various diameter culvert sections or old metal wheels. A simple triangular shape can be made of wood to frame a window, like shown in the photo.

In addition to stiffening door and window openings with frames, it is a good idea to drive vertical metal rods or rebar stakes through the bags near the edge of the opening in such a way that they avoid hitting any anchor plates within the walls. This stake can eventually be incorporated into the bond beam at the top of the wall.

I might caution you that with earthbag domes you need to be careful not to riddle them with too many windows or doors. Because domes rely on the barbed wire for the tensile strength of the walls, too many perforations can compromise this and introduce weaknesses into the wall.

Sometimes it is not convenient to use openable windows with earthbag projects, so some other way to introduce good ventilation may be necessary. I have done this by using vent pipes placed in strategic places, both low and high within the structure. A section of most any large diameter pipe can serve this purpose; I have used both metal and plastic for this. Such a vent placed at the apex of a dome can create a considerable draft when some inlet air vent is opened as well. One simple way to provide vent closures for these is to use an inflated ball that fits the diameter of the pipe.

While on the topic of openings, I might mention that once a wall is completed, it is rather difficult to go back and retrofit a wall with either a door or window. Cutting through an earthbag wall can be a messy and even hazardous venture. For this reason, I advise you to frame in any door or window spaces that you expect you may need at some future time during the initial construction phase. These can be finished so that they may not be noticeable, but you will know they are waiting there if necessary.

Arches

The use of arches can be an effective and elegant way to create and stabilize wall openings. I have seen a variety of ways of doing this, but almost always they employ some form of temporary support while building the arch. These arch supports can be built from most any rigid material in the shape that you want the final arch to be. Once the support is released it is available for use in some other location.

The above arch form was made from two pieces of plywood cut to a half-round shape and connected together with short lengths of 2X4 inch wood strips. It was then clamped to the top of the door buck that was already in place.

It is most convenient if the form is initially secured in such a way that it is easy to knock out some spacers that will allow the form to lower enough to be able to pull it out and away from the arched bags. Otherwise, the weight and friction of the bags on the form can make this difficult.

I have found that half circular arches work fine for spans up to about three feet, but much wider than that they seem vulnerable to collapse. For wider spans up to six feet I think that the pointed gothic arch form is more secure.

A simple radial pattern of stacking the bags, like that shown in the first photo is common. In doing this it is obviously necessary to fasten the top of the bags very securely so there is no possibility of spillage. The way to stack the bags is alternately from both sides until there is space for one last "capstone" bag, which must be firmly tamped into place to assure that compression won't later dislodge it.

Before attempting to remove an arch form, it is best to build up the walls on both sides of it to the point where there is no possibility of any sideways movement of the bags comprising the arch. In fact, if the arch is built along with the wall, it is possible to run the barbed wire between the arch bags and the wall bags, thus securing the whole assembly as a unit.

You will notice that the photo to the left shows a different pattern of stacking bags. This what I call a "double crosshatch" pattern, and it resulted from much experimentation in trying to make an arch spanning six feet. I used a set of miniature bags I had made to come up with the concept. Basically alternating courses of two bags placed side by side and oriented in a # pattern creates a much more solid arch. In fact I found that, as shown in the model above, such an arch can remain unsupported by lateral walls.

When using the long tubular bags filled with fully stabilized material, it is possible to make arches in a very different way. These still utilize a form to build the arch over, but the method can be simplified considerably. The photos show approaches that create arches of the same thickness as the wall itself, or even adding a sort of eyebrow to protect the window. Either the single or double bag method can also create eyebrows over the opening.

Bond Beams

Bond beams are a way to stiffen a wall at the junction of the wall and the roof, or the wall and a second floor or loft. These are places where it is necessary to connect the wall to other kinds of materials and there is a need for absolute rigidity. Bond beams also serve to stabilize the wall itself, firming up the entire structure.

The most common bond beam is made with reinforced concrete that is formed to match the exact shape of the wall. If any vertical steel stakes have been driven into the wall to help stiffen it, these stakes can protrude above the top bags so that they also get incorporated into the concrete bond beam;

this creates a very strong matrix for the entire structure. At the time of pouring the concrete, J-bolts can be embedded for eventual connection to a top plate for the roof or floor joists.

With straight walls it is possible to make the bond beam with lumber that has been attached to the wall with steel rods driven into the wall at intervals. If the top of the rods are bent over and they are driven through pre-drilled holes at various angles, this can connect the bond beam securely.

I have come up with another way to make bond beams for straight-sided buildings that also provides some hurricane and earthquake protection for the walls and the roof framing. At the same time this method will automatically provide strong lintels over doors and windows.

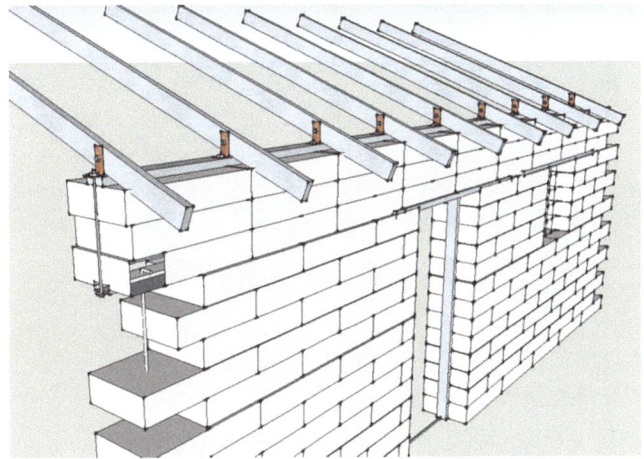

The idea is that during construction, once you have arrived at the height where you are at the level of the top of any door or window (presuming that these are the same height), you lay down a piece of hollow, rectangular-section steel tubing right on top of that last row of earthbags. It is also possible to do this with pieces of wood by using somewhat larger dimensions, but I prefer metal because it is stronger and more reliable in its characteristics. It should be as long as the wall is, going from the center of one corner to the center of the other corner. In most localities you can purchase such tubing up to 6 meters (20 feet) long, and two pieces can be strapped together if necessary, using connection plates that are either welded or bolted in place. This tubing can be various sizes, depending on how long the wall is, but I recommend about 1 1/2" X 4" in general.

It would be a good idea to have made this area as level as possible, through tamping or even shimming some bags, so that the steel beam will lie as level as it can. Before putting this first piece of steel in place, it should be pre-drilled with 1/2" holes at 1 foot intervals all the way through both sides of the metal in the center of the long dimension.

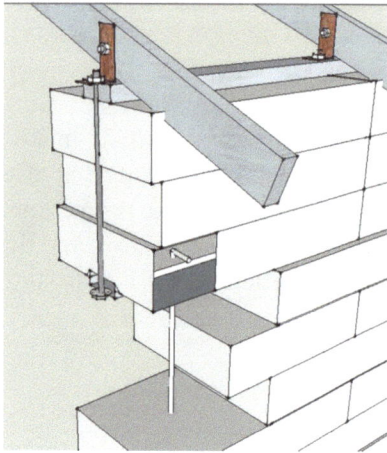

If you look at the above cross-section detail you can see that there is a piece of 3/8" rebar about 2 feet long with one end bent over 90 degrees. Such pieces of rebar can be pounded down through every other hole and into the bags below. But don't pound them all the way down yet, because you also want to install some 2 foot sections of 1/2" threaded rod (sometime called "all-thread") sticking up vertically in each of the empty holes that are left. These need to be secured with steel washers and nuts underneath the beam, so they can't be pulled out. Once all of the pieces of threaded rods are in place, you can finish pounding down all of the rebar anchors. Now the whole assembly should remain fixed securely in place.

Wherever the threaded rods are over doors or windows you may need to put a nut on the rod on top of the beam so that it won't fall through the hole. Also, the lower washer and nut can be recessed into the beam by drilling a large enough hole on the lower side of the beam to do so. This will allow other window or door assemblies to be joined flush with the beam.

Now you can place some extra pieces of the same type of tubular metal over the door and window openings on either side of the original beam, so that they are long enough to extend maybe 1 1/2 feet on either side of the opening. These can also be pinned

into place with similar rebar pins. This will become a platform over which more earthbags will be placed.

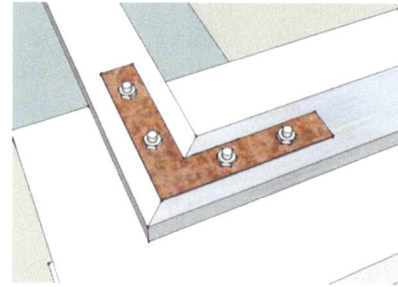

At the corners where two bond beams meet, the metal beams can be connected rigidly with 90 degree metal brackets on either side of each beam, through-bolted in a similar manner. This will make the entire structure integrally connected, which should withstand considerable force from earthquakes or wind.

At this point you are ready to start laying more earthbags. These should be filled so that they will be 2 feet long when tamped into place. This may mean that they will need to be hemmed or stitched at the top, if there is not enough material to fold over and seal them that way. They will be placed directly between the threaded rods and tamped thoroughly into place. It might be possible to pierce the subsequent row of bags with the threaded rods in order to maintain the staggered, brick-like layering of bags, but it will be easier to just place them above each other and between the rods. Because these bags will be eventually clamped together to form the bond beam, it doesn't really matter much whether they are staggered or not. In most cases, three rows of bags can be arranged this way, but depending on the intended height of the wall, you can also lay fewer or more rows, as long as the threaded rods are long enough to extend above the upper beam.

This upper steel beam needs to be prepared with 1/2" holes drilled to match exactly the pattern of the lower one so that it can be placed in the middle of the topmost bags with the ends of the threaded rods protruding all the way through. In this case there is no real need to also pound rebar pins through the bags, since this whole assembly will be clamped tight as a unit, so fewer holes need to be drilled through the upper beam.

Before the washers and nuts are put onto the rods, you want to position metal L-brackets wherever there will be rafters or joists. These brackets will connect these roof members to the bond beam in a solid, yet flexible manner. As you tighten down the nuts on all of the threaded rods, be sure to check the level of the beam, making sure that it becomes as level as possible, so the roof itself will be level. It may be necessary to tighten some of them more than others. You want this whole assembly to be clamped tightly together so that there is no chance of any of the bags becoming dislodged, but there is no reason to over tighten them either; you don't want to overly bend or stress the metal.

Plaster

In preparing a wall for plastering, you should try to get the surface all into the same plane as much as possible. This would be the time to pound in any protruding bag corners and flatten any bags that stick out noticeably. You can also take a putty knife or screw driver and tuck in any loose bag material that might interfere with there being a good bond between the plaster and the wall.

In most situations the use of plaster mesh is a good idea; mesh will help hold the plaster in place while it is curing, and will also help keep it there over time. Chicken wire (either 1 or 2 inch wire works), stucco mesh, and even synthetic fish netting has been used for this purpose.

One way to fix the mesh to the wall is with home-made U-shaped staples. These can be cut from wire that is stiff enough to be able to pound them into place with a hammer. Prongs that measure 3 or 4

inches long should hold the mesh onto the wall well enough.

Plaster is usually applied in two or three coats, with the first one left rough enough to provide good "tooth" for the next one. The last coat would be the finish or smooth coat. One way to assure that the first coat gets well adhered to the wall beyond the mesh, is to actually throw it with the trowel at the wall. If you aim towards the crevices between the bags, this is where the best opportunity is for the plaster to grab onto the wall.

Interior plaster can be most anything that covers the wall well that you want to live with. This could be an earthen plaster (sand and clay), lime, cement stucco, or even papercrete. A combination of these might also work; with one project (pictured above), I used an initial coat of papercrete with a finish coat of white lime for a nice bright finish.

The exterior plaster is best stabilized with some cement or lime to protect the finish from weathering too much, especially if it is not protected by wide roof eaves. In general it is best that the plaster breathes some, so if any moisture manages to enter the wall it can dissipate eventually.

With domes it is absolutely necessary to provide a waterproof coating to avoid water entering the building and compromising the integrity of the dome or promoting the growth of mold. For this reason I usually recommend cement stucco on the dome exterior. You can add some latex to the stucco mix that helps with making it waterproof. Then, after the stucco has cured, an exterior roof paint can be applied for added protection.

There is much more that can be said about plastering; see the resources that are focused specifically about this.

Roofs

Most any conventional roof system can be used over an earthbag building. Obviously, a design that includes rounded or domed forms with rectilinear ones can present more challenges to roof design. I prefer pitched roofs rather than flat (or nearly flat) roofs; they usually do a better job of shedding moisture and keeping it away from the walls.

With the exception of domes and very small vaults, earthbags cannot be used to create a roof. It is possible to use earthbags filled with insulating materials to insulate other roof systems, and I have done this a few times. In the photo the earthbags are filled with scoria, a lightweight natural insulating material.

In the discussion about bond beams I mentioned some ways to attach the roof framing members to the bond beam. For the most part, these details resemble those used with any other wall system, where there is a top plate that can be used to attach rafters, trusses, etc. Sometimes these are secured with wind resistant connectors, where this might be a threat.

Floors

Most earthbag project have floors at or near the grade of the property, with perhaps no more than a step up. A concrete pad is certainly one flooring option, but is not the only one. The floor could also be made with flagstone, brick, pavers, poured adobe or rammed earth. Carpet could be laid over any of these, but tile would need a solid concrete base most likely. The photo shows a combination of flagstone on the right with poured adobe scored to appear like stone; an oil finish is being applied to both.

It is almost always a good idea to put some insulation down before making the floor over it. This will isolate the floor from the earth below, which would otherwise tend to siphon off the warmth and bleed energy. It is possible to use commercial rigid foam insulation for this purpose, but a more natural alternative that I have used is crushed scoria, a lightweight volcanic stone.

If you want a raised floor with a crawl space beneath it, this is also possible. To do this it would be good to create a bond beam below the floor level where a plate can be made to secure the floor to it. Then standard floor joists and other flooring materials can be added. More earthbags can be stuffed between the joists to continue with the wall that goes up.

Utilities

How do you handle electrical and plumbing circuits in an earthbag house?

Electrical wire can be routed between the bags before they get plastered, either with conduit or using UF wire accepted for direct burial in the plaster. If the wire or conduit is tucked into the crevasse between the bags it will not interfere with the application of the plaster.

To install the electrical boxes you can simply drive some long pointed wooden stakes into the bags where you want them and leave enough sticking out to screw the boxes to. With fairly loose fill this is easy to do and they are plenty strong. This may be harder to do with some soils, especially if stabilized. Once the stakes are driven in they are amazingly firm and do not wobble, and of course the plaster holds them even better.

Often it is easier to route plumbing into wood framed partition walls inside the house, and otherwise route drains and such under the floor (as shown above). In my earthbag house I brought the primary water line in below frost level and then up to connect with plumbing in a framed interior wall. This avoids any issues with freezing pipes. You can run water lines in the cracks between bags.

If frost is not an issue, then it would be possible to just poke the pipe directly through the wall while you are building it, or even pound a section of steel pipe through after the fact. Or you can leave larger diameter pipe in appropriate places to serve as chases for pipe later on.

The black water from the toilet needs to drain to an appropriate septic tank or sewer line. The shower and sinks drain could be plumbed into a gray-water tank for possible re-use if you want.

Hanging Cabinets, etc.

How do you attach cabinets and such to an earthbag wall?

The answer, to some extent, depends upon what you fill the bags with. If you use an adobe-like soil that contains some clay, then you can actually use very long screw that will hold quite a bit of weight. With other, looser soil or material, you need to use another strategy.

Earthbag walls can support a great deal of weight if the attachments are done right. You can embed wood or steel into the wall where you want to hang cabinets. This can be done either at the time of building the wall, or it can be done later by simply driving stakes into the wall. This might be easier done in places where there is already a slight void, like between bags or courses of bags.

You can easily pound long sections of threaded rods all the way through bags, and then bolt sections of wood (even 2" X 4" s) on both sides, that are very secure. If they are long enough, a whole row of cabinets can be hung on them. Piercing the earthbags, even with loose material, is not a problem.

Peaceful Valley

My first hands-on experience of building with earthbags was soon after we bought the property in Colorado where we wanted to park our bus home. The street was called Peaceful Way, so we decided to call our property "Peaceful Valley," as there was a small waterway down the middle of it. We had gotten permission from the property owners association to build a house with earthbags, but I wanted to first gain some experience on a small trial structure.

We decided to make a small earthbag dome, just using the local soil (basically sand) to fill the bags. We figured that we could use the building for storage or a garden shed eventually, so it didn't really need to be insulated.

Riceland

Most of the misprinted polypropylene bags that we bought were marked "Riceland," a brand of rice, so we started calling this little dome Riceland. There were no books available at that time (1996) to guide me with how to build this way, but I thought how hard could it be to fill and stack bags with barbed wire between them? I had already seen several successful earthbag domes, so I had some idea of the appropriate shape.

We selected a site not too far from where we planned to build the house and leveled an area large enough for the dome. I placed a stake in the center of the space and used a string as a 7 foot radius to scribe a 14 foot diameter (interior) circle. Another circle

about a foot and a half larger in radius described the outside of the dome.

Then we dug a trench about a foot deep between the circular lines, added an entrance space with flanking buttresses, and were ready to fill the trench with rubble for the foundation. We would have gone further down below the frost level (about 5 feet in that region) but since the sand drained so well it seemed pointless.

Soon I was filling the bags with the sand I had piled up, stacking them on the wall and putting the barbed wire between the courses. I kept the wall covered with tarps when I wasn't working on it. How exciting it was to see this building materialize, primarily from the earth beneath it!

I used a 14 foot plastic pole as a radius for the arc that defined the curve of the wall going up. I would place this pole at the base of the wall and then pass it through the imaginary center axis of the dome, checking the accuracy of where I had placed the bags. I did this every time I completed one course, in several places around the wall. I could have set up a mechanical compass arrangement to do this, but I liked the simplicity of doing it this way. At first the wall rose nearly vertically, so the curvature wasn't noticed until it was about 3 feet high.

We found some culvert couplers that we used as forms to create round windows in this little dome. They were just as wide as the bags and got solidly locked into the wall as the bags pressed against the corrugated surface.

You might notice that with this dome I was tying baling twine around the bags as well as placing the barbed wire between them. This was an attempt to make the wall even more monolithic, and I thought that the extra twine would help hold the plaster to the wall. I later dispensed with this, deeming it unnecessary.

One day while I was happily carrying buckets of sand up a ladder to fill the bags in place, my eye caught a discrepancy in the perfectly circular aspect of the top row of bags. I thought this was strange since I was sure I had checked that course with my pole. As I stood on top of the wall I felt movement beneath me and I could see that the wall was caving in! I immediately jumped outside the dome to be safe and watched as almost the entire structure imploded to the ground. It was like watching a slow motion wave in action, proceeding from one side of the wall around to the other.

Yikes! I was safe, but it was a major calamity; a tangled mess of bags, sand, barbed wire, bent ladder and

culvert couplers. The buttresses at the doorway kept that part from collapsing, and the wall up to about a yard high was OK. But what had gone wrong?

It took days for me to clean up the mess, and my confidence was severely shaken. I had plenty of time to ponder the problem and ultimately realized that my mistake was to use the native sand, which was very fine and slippery... a true shape shifter. Basically, once I got high enough up the wall, gravity dictated that it was going to pull the wall down by shifting the sand in the bags. This is why it is so important to use a fill material that will consolidate into a more solid mass when erecting a dome. Now I know!

My intention all along was to use crushed scoria to fill the bags for our dome home, because it is lightweight, mined locally, and provides fairly good insulation due to all of the trapped air in the voids of this volcanic stone. So at this point with Riceland, we decided to switch to filling the bags with scoria and see if it would actually work well as a fill. But first I made a tiny dome with the scoria to test the theory. The photo shows me smiling inside the completed test dome, and I was confident enough to proceed with reconstructing Riceland.

Working with the scoria was actually much easier, due to its lighter weight. I could fill the bags on the ground and easily carry them to the wall, since each bag only weighed about 35 pounds. I carefully tamped the courses into place to get the loose scoria to pack into a kind of block that was solid enough to hold its shape. It wasn't long before I got back to the height of where it was at the time of the collapse, and all was fine.

My first attempt at making the buttresses surrounding the doorway, using a stack of single bags on top of each other, was too wobbly. So I tried using this pattern of two bags placed side by side in an alternating crosshatch pattern, and this was much more stable. As I was building the buttresses I inserted wooden blocks with half inch threaded rod bolted through them, and the rod sticking out between the bags.

This allowed me to eventually fasten the wooden door frame securely to the buttress.

When I got up to the height of the top of the door it was time to set up a form for an arched window over

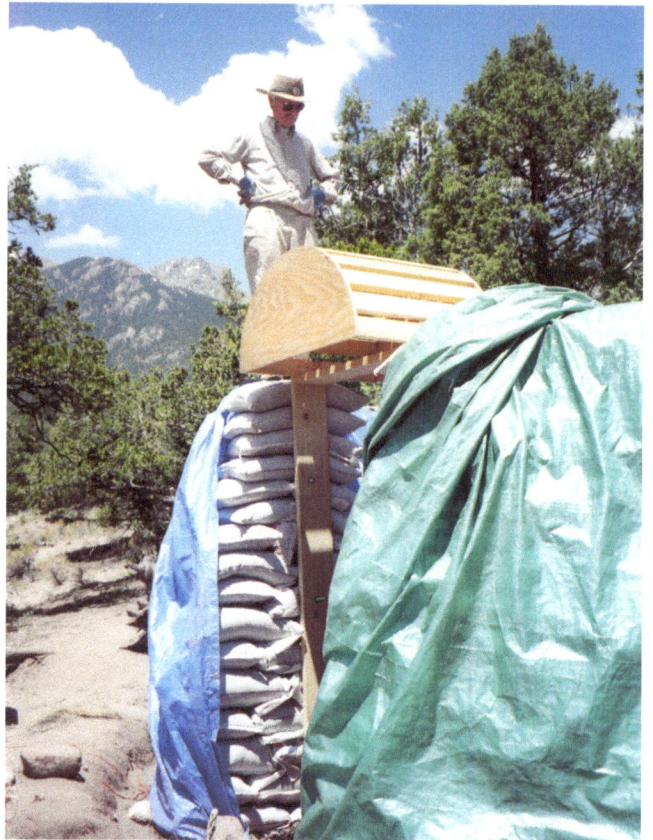

the door. I proceeded to fashion the arch as described earlier in the section about building arches, using single bags laid over the form.

The plan was to build a half loft in the upper part of the dome that could be used for sleeping or additional storage space. I framed this loft by simply laying 2 X 6 inch joists all the way across the dome and resting them on the top of the wall. I used wooden shims to assure that the loft was level and in one plane. Then I filled in the spaces between the joists with more bags of scoria. I noticed that as soon as I had the loft framing locked into place, the whole structure became more rigid and didn't vibrate as much when I walked around on the top bags.

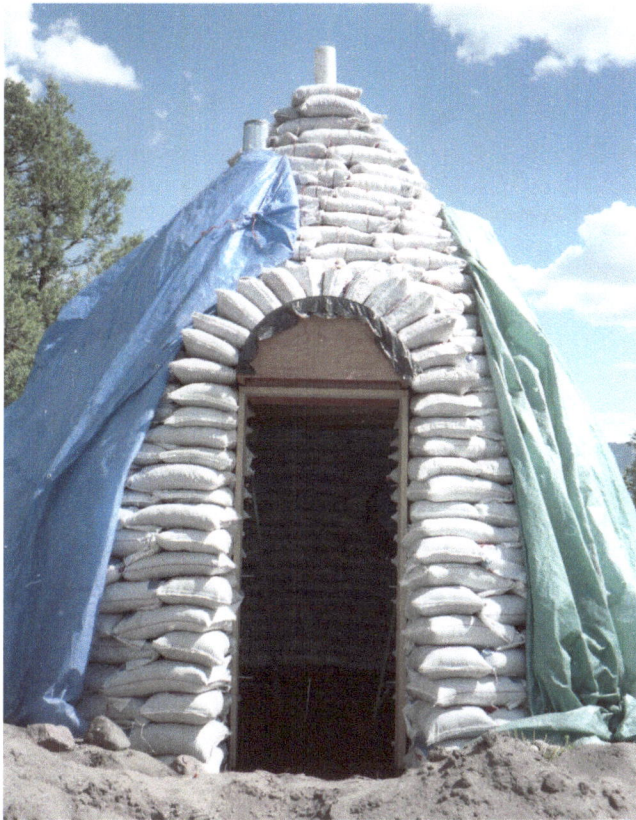

As I neared completion of the top of the dome I inserted a couple of vents. The first was a section of insulated stove pipe for an eventual wood stove if needed. The other was a section of 8 inch PVC pipe to serve as an air vent right at the apex. How satisfying it was to place those final bags and have the dome completed!

Around the time that we were building Riceland I had taken a workshop with Mike McCain, one of the inventors of papercrete, and I was intrigued with its potential as a plaster over earthbags. Papercrete is essentially scrap paper that has been turned into a pulp, mixed with Portland cement, and allowed to cure.

It is necessary to somehow mechanically mix the paper slurry to return the fibers to a pulp and mix in the cement. This can be done in a kitchen blender, but to make enough papercrete to plaster an entire dome would require a huge industrial blender. So I made one using a 55 gallon plastic drum, a threaded rod spindle suspended down the middle of it with bushings at either end to keep it stable. At the lower end of the rod I fabricated a steel cutting blade, and on

top, above the barrel, I attached a small electric motor. I cut a hole in the top of the barrel large enough to insert the paper and cement, and at the bottom I put in a 4 inch drain with a threaded plug. Then I was set to give the thing a whirl.

First I filled the barrel about half full of water, then I started to drop strips of torn up newspaper that had been soaking in water over night. I found that if I didn't feed it too quickly the motor could handle shredding it into a slurry. The more paper I added, the thicker the slurry got. When it was getting pretty thick, I would add about one large shovel full of dry Portland cement and let it thoroughly mix.

This slurry then needed to be drained of excess water to make the wet papercrete thick enough to be able to apply it as a plaster. I did this by dumping it into a drain box set up below the drain plug in the mixer. You can see this drain box on its side in the photo. The bottom of the box was a synthetic mesh screen that was fine enough to keep the paper fibers from passing through, but the water would just seep away. Interestingly, this excess water was perfectly clear, as the paper fiber held all of the cement particles like a filter.

After the water had drained for about half an hour or so, the papercrete was ready to apply. We would take bucketfuls of the stuff over to the wall and place it by rubber gloved hands directly onto the bags. It was a very plastic, clay-like substance that was easy to manipulate this way.

Above Rosana was applying the papercrete to the outside of Riceland. We didn't use any wire mesh for plaster at this point, and found that it was sufficiently adhered when it was pushed into all of the crevasses between the bags.

It takes papercrete at least a week to cure as it slowly dries out. Then if it gets wet again it will absorb a great deal of moisture, rather like a sponge. In most applications this can make it problematic as a plaster, but in this case, with the bags of scoria, we found that the papercrete would not pass the moisture through

the wall to the inside; it would simply get damp and then dry out to the atmosphere, especially in that rather arid Colorado climate. Also, interestingly, the papercrete didn't seem to expand or contract with moisture or freeze/thaw cycles.

When my sister and her son visited I put them to work applying papercrete to the very top of the dome. You can tell that the wet papercrete is darker than after it cures some.

I bought quite a bit of double pane glass as seconds rather cheaply from local glass shops; they end up with lots of this as customer returns or miss-sized glass. All I cared was that the glass was big enough to cover the intended opening, so the exact size didn't matter. Above I was fitting the glass over the opening while the papercrete was still wet, so that I could score around the glass and dig out enough papercrete to embed it in place. Later, after the papercrete had cured I would caulk around the glass.

Bedroom

Having successfully completed one small dome, Rosana and I felt confident enough to proceed with beginning the construction of our actual house. We waited until the next spring to embark on this, retreating to a warmer southern region to winter in our bus home.

This time we started right out filling the bags with scoria. In fact, we realized that, given how well the native sand drains, there was really no need for the

rubble trench foundation. Instead, we spread about 6 inches of scoria (the red stone you can see in the above picture) over the entire footprint of the dome. We did this primarily to help insulate the floor itself from the ground below.

Rather than placing tarps over the walls, this time we stretched tarps over the entire dome to create a shade structure. This served well, except in windy weather we often had to make repairs, so it may have created more work for us.

In the photo you can see someone fitting a bag over the metal funnel (part of a chicken feeder) that we used to help fill the bags. The rows of bags behind him are already filled with scoria and waiting to go up on the wall.

For this bedroom dome we made the interior diameter 16 feet, a little larger than Riceland. It also had a loft framed over part of it with bags of scoria placed between the joists. A culvert coupler served as a window opening. Part of the exterior wall had already been plastered with papercrete.

On the far side you can see a very large arch, spanning 6 feet, that we tried to make by stacking single bags over a temporary form that was made by just stacking more bags underneath it in the shape that we wanted. We soon discovered that we made several mistakes in doing this. The first mistake was thinking that single bags forming a semicircular arch that

spans 6 feet would be sufficiently strong to hold its shape.

As you can see in the above photo, we had a massive failure of that arch, causing the adjacent walls that were connected to it to collapse. Obviously, that method of making an arch spanning that distance needed to be improved upon.

It was at this point that I came up with the double crosshatch method of forming an arch, as suggested earlier in my discussion about making arches. This was actually an extension of the idea of making the buttresses that flanked the door by also using double crosshatch bags. These two approaches work well together, since the arch is provided with a very solid and wide platform to be launched from.

In addition to doing this, I made a new wooden arch form that was more of a Gothic, pointed arch. The combination of these two changes created a very secure arch indeed, and I used this same method in several other locations while building this house.

We wanted an opening that spanned 6 feet because our plan called for a large sliding glass door in the

bedroom to enhance the passive solar heating potential for that room. We bought commercial vinyl doors and a half-round window to match it and embedded these in the papercrete plaster.

We also wanted an openable window in the bedroom for ventilation, so we bought a matching small sliding window with a half-round above it that is visible left of the door in the photo below. Like with Riceland I placed an 8 inch PVC pipe vent at the very top of the dome as an exit air vent.

By the time that the snow began to fly we had the bedroom snugly plastered and ready for winter. A three foot wide doorway was prepared that would lead from the bedroom into the rest of the house, but since we needed to leave it over winter, we bagged up

that doorway and put a temporary plaster over it.

Montecito

The next building season brought us to the most complex and challenging portion of this monumental project. This was the large oval dome that would comprise our kitchen/dining/living room/and loft office. It measured roughly 20 feet on the short axis and 30 feet on the long axis. It was positioned about 20 feet away from the bedroom dome, and like the bedroom, would have a six foot glassed entry, as well as several large circular windows for passive solar heat.

Soon after we started the construction we came up with the name "Montecito" for this dome, which means "little mountain" in Spanish, because we realized that the dome itself would be a veritable mountain of bags.

Montecito would be substantially bermed into the south-facing slope, and you can see in the photo below how the leveled building pad has left a bank of native sand around parts of the perimeter. We hired an excavator to do the digging this time to speed the project along. On the far right you can see another room that was dug out at the same time that would eventually become our pantry. In the distance the bedroom and our bus home are visible.

We foolishly made a huge tent-like shade structure

over the building area, but the wind made quick work of demolishing it so we went back to putting tarps over the walls themselves.

The elliptical footprint was broken by four doors leading to all four directions. Each of these openings would be framed by hefty double bagged buttresses.

We found some antique steel wheels that had been parts of farm equipment and had very wide rims that could actually support some bags placed on top, and we used these for decorative window supports in the south-facing direction.

We used the same arch support that had been successful in the bedroom to form the arch over the entry. In the above photo you can also see the log ends of several large log supports (vigas) for the loft. As with the other domes, as soon as these vigas were locked into place, the entire structure become much firmer while working on it. I tarred the exposed ends of the logs and they were flush with the bags so that they would eventually get covered by the papercrete plaster. You can see these as black dots in the above photo.

Above is pictured the entry into the pantry next to the kitchen with the vigas ready to support the loft over that area. I harvested these logs as dead standing timber with a firewood permit from the local National Forest, and then debarked them with a draw knife.

The view above shows the main street entrance to the house. You will notice that there are a couple of vigas that are set perpendicular to the others that extend over to the opposite wall. I did this to help stabilize that part of the structure.

Another viga connected the bedroom to Montecito; this would eventually be used as part of the supporting structure for the midsection of the house.

At this point in the construction, all seemed to be progressing very well indeed, with everything feeling quite solid, and we were happy campers, if a bit tired from all of the labor. We did have some help from friends at times, especially Peter B. Rice (pictured above), who spent several summers with us working as our "teenage slave" to gain work experience. Rosana helped when there were things that she felt comfortable doing, like filling bags with the scoria. But the bulk of the construction was done with my own two hands; it is a good thing that I thoroughly enjoy using my body and mind this way.

For the second story above the loft of Montecito I felt that I needed to create some sort of temporary framework to guide the shape of the bag walls. So I did this by first erecting a tripod that would support a boat-like structure that would somewhat resemble the oval shape at the top. I connected 2 X 6 inch struts from this down to the existing perimeter of the wall. The idea was that I would use this while building, and then remove it entirely once the dome was complete.

Soon I was happily stacking bags of scoria again; the bags were light enough that I could carry them up the ladder to find their place on the wall. We used several smaller antique wagon wheels for the window openings above the loft.

As Montecito gained weight I noticed a few somewhat troubling aberrations in the form of the walls. One was in an area below the loft on the north side where there was a tendency for the wall to bulge outward. In the photo below you can see how I had used a log coupled with a hydraulic jack to try to push it back into shape. Eventually I decided to alleviate the downward pressure in that region by installing a permanent vertical pole supporting two of the loft vigas.

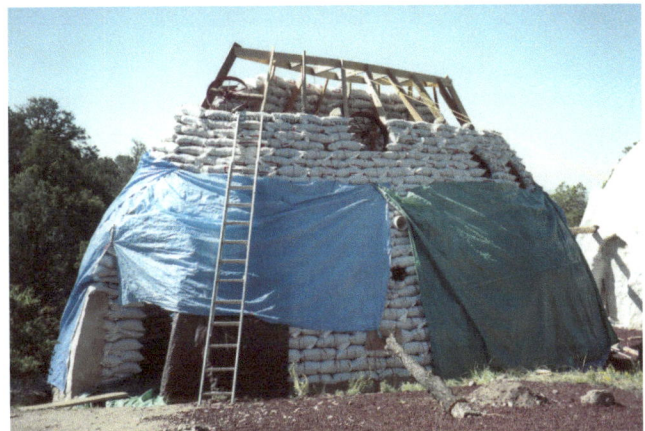

This vertical support eventually became part of the structure for a set of shelves. In the above photo you can see how the entrance from the east came into the house onto a landing, and from there some simple steps went up to the loft. The bags that created the landing were filled with the native sand, since that area did not need to be insulated, and in fact the thermal performance of the house would benefit from there being more thermal mass inside. I did this in several other places, such as in parts of the buttresses.

I persevered with stacking bags up to the very top of the temporary form, and even installed a couple of vent pipes at the top. Then I noticed something very troubling indeed. The relatively flat sections of the walls, especially on the north side, were pressing heavily on the temporary guiding framework. The more I analyzed the situation, the more I realized that if I removed those supporting 2 X 6's the whole wall might just collapse! In other words, the oval shape that I was attempting to create with earthbags was

inherently unstable. With circular domes, all of the forces around the circle are in equilibrium, but with this ellipse, the long sides exert more pressure than the shorter ends. This effect was exaggerated by the boat-like shape I had created at the top, so that the net effect was that those long walls might just come tumbling down, unless they were somehow held in place.

I spent a rather sleepless night once I realized all of this, and by morning I had come to the conclusion that my best recourse was to remove the entire upper level and start over again with a rigid and permanent support structure above the loft. This was a rather depressing thought, partly because I knew that winter was just around the corner and I wanted to get Montecito sealed up before then.

So I carefully started to dismantle several week's worth of work, dropping the bags full of scoria down to the floor below the loft. Most of the bags survived their fall and were reusable. I carefully rolled up the barbed wire for reuse later.

For a permanent support framework, I first fabricated an oval hoop of metal that was spanned with some wooden poles to hold its shape. This metal band would be held up near the top of the dome with radiating poles descending to the perimeter of the bag wall at loft level. Each pole was attached to the metal band with a lag bolt. At the base the pole was either attached to one of the vigas for the loft, or it was attached to a wooden plate that was extended out from the bag wall itself. As the photo shows, this plate was pinned into place in the wall with a section of rebar.

As an added measure of caution, I drilled holes through each pole about 4 feet up from its base in such a way that I could thread a heavy duty wire cable around the entire structure, as one would do with a yurt to keep the roof rafters from expanding outward. Before I tightened and secured this cable, I fixed some horizontal poles between each of the vertical ones. These can be seen in the photos to the right.

I had the foresight to wrap all of the wooden poles with industrial clear plastic wrap so that it would protect the wood from all of the plaster that I knew would eventually be slathered up there to cover the bags between the poles. I figured that I could easily cut this away with a knife once the plastering was finished, and the poles would be pristine, and this did work out well.

Whenever I had some extra help I put folks to work hoisting up the old bags from the heap on the floor with a rope and pulley arrangement, so that I could place them in the wall above.

Before long we had managed to get the project back to the point where I discovered the weakness in my original plan and had to regroup. This time I felt much more confident in the enduring stability of the structure. And with the cable around the perimeter

39

of the upper framework, I felt that the building could even survive a small earthquake.

Ever since this experience I have cautioned people that earthbag domes are best kept to circular structures. I feel that the risk of imbalance that we experienced with Montecito is best avoided entirely. And even with circular domes I feel that about 20 feet in diameter is the largest that can be safely done.

Around the time that we started building Montecito I realized that the project would go much faster if I were able to make the papercrete plaster in greater quantities. Mike McCain, the papercrete master, had invented a truly industrial mixer that he called a tow mixer, and I enlisted his help in fabricating one for me. It is really a rather simple idea of using the rear axel of a small pickup truck and placing the drive connection pointing upwards so that a lawn mower blade can be attached to it. Around this blade is secured a large tank, like the stock tank pictured above. A separate tow bar and hitch is welded to the axel so that when the mixer is pulled behind a vehicle, the blade is forced to turn with tremendous power. All it would take is the equivalence of one pass around the block at slow speed, and by the time you returned the papercrete would be completely mixed and ready to dump into the drain box.

I used this mixer to produce enough papercrete to cover the completed Montecito, and barely got the job done before winter. As with the bedroom the previous year, I temporarily filled in some of the doorways with earthbags.

You will notice three vents exiting the peak of Montecito. The two on either side are air vents, and the central one is for a wood stove that would be located

near the middle of the room. The windows in the picture above are waiting to be covered with glass that would be embedded in fresh papercrete. Fortunately papercrete is stable enough dimensionally that it is safe to do this; with many plasters, thermal expansion might break the glass.

Midsection

The next phase of construction was to join Montecito to the bedroom dome with a connecting space that would serve many functions. On the lower level would be a greenhouse, bathroom, utility space, and above that would be a small office.

My plan called for a section of a sphere on the north that would basically rest upon the two domes to support it. The south side would be framed with wood to easily provide glazing for the greenhouse, as well as a large flat roof for various solar panels.

To test my theory that it would be possible to create such a section of a sphere using earthbags, I pulled out my little kit of miniature earthbags and started to stack them between two dome-like mounds of papercrete. The photo shows the result of this, and it all seemed like it was stable enough that it was worth a try at full scale.

In reality, the bag wall proceeded fairly easily up to the first story, mainly because this part was nearly vertical. The back of the wall to the north was going to be substantially bermed, so the lower bags were filled with soil for thermal mass, and then scoria was placed up against them for insulation. An apron of black plastic was put into place to protect it all from moisture before it got backfilled.

I stabilized the back wall further by connecting floor/ceiling joists across to the large viga that had already been secured between the two domes. A couple of vertical posts helped support this platform.

The second story soon became more of a challenge as the wall curved further inward; gravity was working against me at this point. It required periodic braces to keep the wall from toppling. Two round culvert coupler windows were also braced into place and the bags were stacked around them.

When the wall arrived at the right height to attach rafters for the roof, I connected these to the viga at the base and where they intersected the bag wall, I pounded long rebar stakes through the rafters and deep into the bag wall. This helped to freeze the wall where I wanted it, as well as secure the rafters in place.

By the time I got all of the rafters positioned, the back wall was able to stand on its own without the braces, however, I did install a few permanent braces just for safety's sake.

To prepare the roof to accept the metal roofing I planned to install, all I needed to do was nail some 1 X 4 stringers across the rafters. This was a very steep roof because I wanted it to be the perfect angle for the best performance of solar panels. I also wanted there to be plenty of head room in that upper space.

41

Below the metal roof, I created an extended bay for a greenhouse bed. This would be right next to the kitchen, convenient for fetching fresh greens. The central part of the little roof over the greenhouse was also glazed for better growth of the plants. And this part of the roof was hinged so that it could be raised a bit to allow good ventilation. Metal flashing was between the metal roof and the papercrete in the domes.

Pantry

The concept for the pantry was that it would be substantially buried underground, and on the north side of the building so that it would rarely receive much direct sunlight and stay cooler. It was basically another small earthbag dome (about 14 feet in diameter) nestled right up against Montecito so that it was really only a little more than half a dome.

Once we had the bags stacked up to about ground level, I decided to provide a conical support structure with poles. This was because I knew that we would be placing more dirt on top of the pantry, and so the pitch on the top needed to be shallow enough that this dirt wouldn't just slide off. The poles were simply resting on the bags and were pinned into them with rebar pins through holes drilled into the wood. At the top there was a small ring for attaching the top of the poles. I ran some concentric wire around the poles to help keep the bags in place.

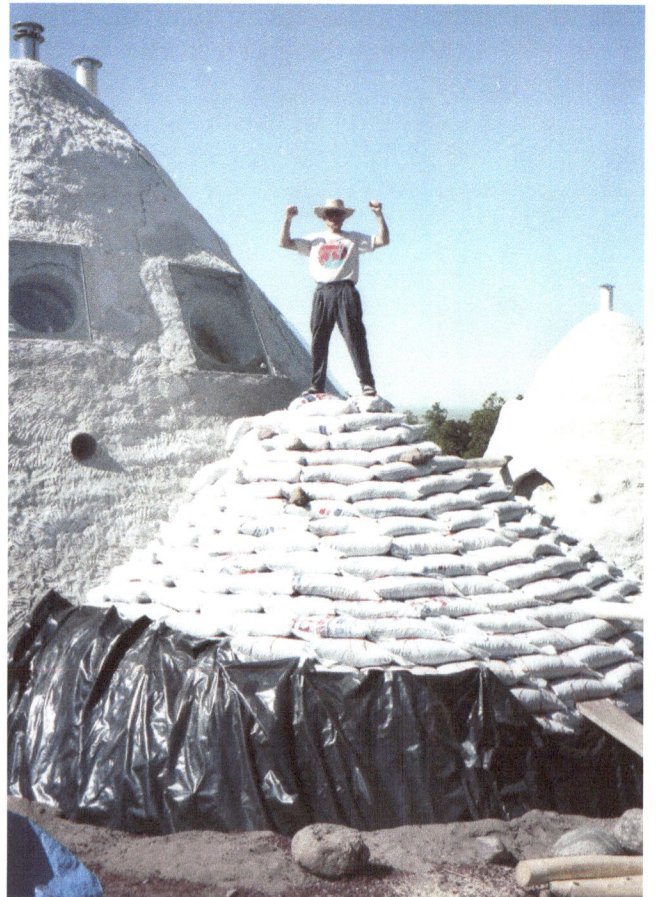

We filled the bags at the base, up to the level of the ground, with the native soil because we wanted it to be coupled directly to the earth, the better to keep it cool. Then we switched to filling them with scoria to help insulate the room from the ambient air outside.

Two layers of 6 mil black plastic were draped over the entire structure before it got backfilled with soil. On the right can be seen a 4 inch PVC vent pipe for inlet air and eventually a 6 inch PVC vent pipe was installed at the apex of the dome.

Mudroom Entry

The final element of the original design for this house was a mudroom entry space leading to the street. The idea was to make a small vault with earthbags, and I was determined to find a way to do this. I had already successfully spanned six feet using the double crosshatch pattern with the bags, so I figured that if I used the same form that I had used for those arches it would work. But I wanted the span at the base to be 8 feet, so I decided to incline the lower part of the vault enough that the span would only be 6 feet higher up. And if these walls were also as thick as the double bags, then it would all match up well. Below you can see how this wall appeared at the point where I placed a frame for a triangular window.

Since the vault was to be much longer than the form for the arch I needed to create a way to slide the form to a new spot once the arch was in place. I did this with some temporary rails that would support the arch form as it was moved forward. This approach worked pretty well, with the thick inclined walls providing enough of a buttressing effect to counteract the outward thrust of the vault.

In the above photo the vault was complete, and a recessed entry door was framed. Peter is in the process of putting papercrete on some small pillars that would support a small bell tower. Right outside the door would be a rope that could be pulled to ring the bell and let us know that somebody was there.

43

This is what the vaulted entry looked like with holiday decorations.

Finished Interior

Creating the shell of this house was only half of the work, as the interior finish details were considerable, as with any house. We greatly enjoyed being able to finally move in. Some of the amenities took several more years to realize, but eventually the house took on the shape and appearance that we dreamed of.

This view of our bedroom shows the earthbag staircase that ascends to the loft area. The entire column serves as thermal mass for this passive solar room. We rarely needed to have supplemental heat in there. The wall finish in the bedroom was the smoothed papercrete that had been given a staining wash of watery latex paint.

The greenhouse bed is on the right and the walkway between the bedroom and the kitchen was laid with flagstone for durability and more thermal mass. On the left was a solar heated hot tub made with a stock water tank lined with local stones. A circulating pump could be turned on to provide a small waterfall down the backing stones into the tub.

Rosana was quite pleased with her cosy office above the greenhouse/bathroom area. You can see some of the permanent braces that help keep that earthbag wall secure.

The kitchen was kind of an odd space, but we made it work with some creative cabinetry.

We created a shower stall in a back corner of the Midsection by lining the space with local stones and tongue and grooved planks.

The door to the right of the kitchen led into the pantry. Behind the curtain were shelves for storage. In a dome it takes some ingenuity to find ways to store things. Inside the pantry we left the earthbags free of plaster, so it became a sort of "truth room." We displayed some of the misprinted bags we had used.

The kitchen and dining area were under the loft in Montecito. At first the central heater was a wood stove, but we discovered that the passive solar heating worked so well it was difficult to regulate the heat so we eventually replaced it with a propane heater.

The interior plaster in Montecito was a thin coating of lime troweled over the papercrete. This produced a bright white finish that was easy to repair with a touch of lime wash.

I found a naturally curved tree branch that was perfect for the balustrade leading up to my office. Besides being my office, the loft in Montecito was our

TV viewing room and occasional guest space.

The square footage (or round feet, as we used to joke) of the entire house, including the loft areas, was around 1300. It ended up taking a full three years of my labor to accomplish, and was exceedingly satisfying. Visitors almost always commented how they immediately felt embraced by the space, with all of the curved features; there were virtually no sharp corners.

This project was nearly complete when the photo at the top on the right was taken. The solar electric panels on the roof provided enough electricity to run all of our lights as well as our refrigerator/freezer. The space below them was reserved for solar thermal panels to heat our domestic water and the hot tub. In the lower right corner of the photo can be seen those thermal panels waiting to be installed.

The total cost of this house, including all of the major appliances but not the land, was about $35,000; this was finished in the year 2000. Then, as fate would have it, about five years later we ended up selling the house when we moved to Mexico for several years. By then, the papercrete finish on the exterior was beginning to show signs of erosion, especially below the windows and on top of the vaulted entry and other flatter areas. At my recommendation, the new owners hired a stucco crew to resurface the entire structure with a tinted cement stucco. The other photos on the right illustrate how this changed the appearance. At the time of this resurfacing, special eyebrows were constructed over the windows, protecting them further. And custom round dual pane windows replaced the original rectangular ones I had installed. I anticipate that this house will still be standing proud a century from now.

Riceland was transformed into a charming guest cabin.

The Pond

Peaceful Valley had a natural water channel dividing it that periodically ran water. We often thought it would be nice to take advantage of this and create a small pond by damming it. Eventually we decided to manifest this pond, and we chose earthbags as a way of making the dam.

I knew that most dams gain their strength by forming a convex curve facing the impounded water, so I mimicked this in my placement of the earthbags. I also knew that it needed to be thickest at the base, so I did this by placing two rows of bags with a space between them that I filled with sand. As the dam gained height I tapered both rows of bags inward so that by the time I was at the top it became just one row of bags.

This is the view of the dam from below. The large stones were used to help stabilize the dam and protect the bags and the plastic that covered them. At the deepest it was about five feet, which was deep enough to keep goldfish over winter.

We lined the entire dam and pond area with black polyethylene to keep the water from just draining away into the sand. To protect the plastic we stacked stones or covered it with gravel.

This pond became one of our favorite places to spend meditative time. It wasn't long before frogs and water loving insect found it. We stocked it with some tiny goldfish that grew and reproduced. All was serene until one day we had deluge of rain that came down so hard and fast that several local streets were nearly washed away. That same brief storm brought so much sand and silt down the arroyo that it overwhelmed the little catch basin we had created to deal with it, and completely filled the entire pond so there was no water left there. The fish were gone, washed further downstream and likely never survived. What a pity... but at least we enjoyed it for those few years before the calamity. And the earthbag dam actually held firmly!

Carriage House

One thing that Peaceful Valley lacked was a good workshop/garage and additional storage space. When we acquired a small RV after selling the bus, we needed a place to store it away from the weather; we needed a carriage house.

After pondering our options for awhile, we decided to order a pre-manufactured steel vault, similar to the old Quonset huts that were popular after the war. We found one deal online that we couldn't refuse: a new 16' X 30' unit, complete with all bolts and parts (but not the end panels) delivered for about $2,000. My concept was that this could be raised up on an earthbag stem wall so that it could also have a second story for a small separate office and more storage space. Furthermore, I figured that we could line the outside of the structure with bags of scoria and it would be as well insulated as the house.

About this time, a friend who had begun construction of a couple of earthbag domes on his nearby land decided to sell the property. Would be buyers wanted the earthbag projects removed, so I offered to help do this in exchange for the bags of scoria. It took a few days of work, but by the time I was done I had a stack of usable bags of scoria sufficient to do the entire carriage house project... all for free.

As an aside, during the demolition of one of the domes I decided to conduct an experiment to see how much soil I could remove from under one section of the wall before it would begin to collapse. To my amazement, as the above photo shows, I had almost entirely removed everything but a small pedestal before it began to separate. The wall was enclosed in wire mesh reinforced stucco which held it all together.

The stem wall for the Carriage House was two bags thick, with a wooden plate attached to the top to connect the steel sections to. Once the steel vault was all bolted into shape and resting on the stem wall, I bolted 2" X 10" wood joists across for the second story floor. These joists served a dual function of also tying the vault so that it couldn't expand with the additional weight of all the bags of scoria on top.

I placed the bags of scoria down into the troughs of each rib, working alternately on both sides to keep the forces balanced as I went up. Then I plastered it with papercrete (later cement stucco was added). This insulation was good enough that, even on very hot days, I could touch the metal inside and it would feel cool.

I built the end walls with recycled materials. The floor was fiber reinforced concrete. The total cost of this 900 square foot building was about $5,000!

The Glorieta

A local spiritual group asked me if I could help them conduct a workshop that would provide some interest and exercise for participants of a week long international conference. Much of what the attendees would be doing was fairly sedentary, so I came up with a concept of having people help build a kind of earthbag monument on the property belonging to the group. We discussed various possible locations and architectural designs and eventually settled on a site where a natural hillside could be terraced in such a way to create seating for a kind of amphitheater. The stage for the amphitheater would also be a relaxing shade structure, a kind of focal point for folks to congregate or meditate. A gazebo or shade structure of this sort is known in Spanish as a "Glorieta," so that is what we decided to call it.

The sand used to fill the bags was dug out from the hillside while forming the terraces of the amphitheater, and the benches along the terraces were also formed with bags of sand. We did place barbed wire between the courses, but made no attempt to stabilized the sand. I felt that with the vertical walls this would be plenty stable... and it has stood the test of time.

Having so many helping hands made fast work of erecting the Glorieta, which was a perfectly round structure with benches built into both sides. Some large descending buttresses opened outward from the stage area in a welcoming fashion.

We assigned various tasks to the volunteers, so that some dug sand from the hillside, while others trans-

ported it via wheelbarrows to the Glorieta. The sand was passed by buckets to those working on the wall who filled and placed the bags, then someone came along with the tamper. Another team measured, cut and placed barbed wire in preparation for the next course of bags.

By the end of the workshop we had all of the bags stacked and some of the lime/cement/sand plaster over them, using chicken wire for mesh. We didn't have time to put up the rafters for the shaded roof (which was to be fabricated by weaving small branches around the rafters, like weaving a basket, so I installed the poles later. We also later hired a professional stucco crew to finish the plastering.

Many participants commented that this experience was the high point of the conference for them. They left with a greater understanding of the possibilities of earthbag building, and a greater appreciation for truly sustainable architecture. After all, we had created an enduring functional and aesthetically pleasing structure, using little more than the soil dug at the site and some poles scavenged as dead standing trees along the nearby watercourse.

Mexican Dome & Model Home

During the time that we lived in Mexico in a small village near Lake Chapala and Guadalajara I became involved with a local Green Group that was promoting sustainable living practices. I made a few presentations about green building, including with earthbags, and this piqued the interest of many folks. One of the coordinators asked me if there might be some sort of practical example of earthbag building that could be done to demonstrate its viability and train some of the locals in the technique. I thought about the possibility and eventually queried a local priest who ran a Catholic boarding school if he would be interested in hosting an earthbag project on the campus of the school. He found the idea intriguing and suggested that I make a presentation to the student body to see if there were sufficient interest.

On the day of the presentation I was a little nervous because my grasp of the Spanish language is limited, but I was able to make myself understood with the help of some large photographs that illustrated my commentary. The teachers and students present all seemed quite interested, and when I asked for a show of hands of how many might participate in working on a project, over half of the hands were raised, including many of the young girls.

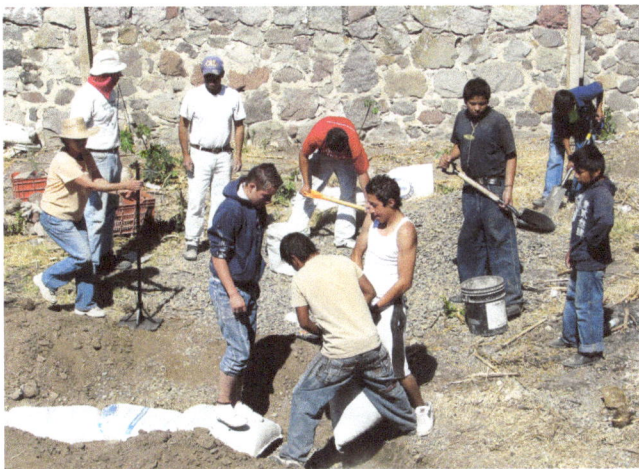

With this encouragement, I went ahead and made arrangements to begin construction of a small dome, similar to Riceland, on the school property. We set aside a few hours on every Saturday morning, when the normal classes were not in session, to embark on this project. Besides the students, I invited members of the Green Group to join us, so it would be a multicultural and mixed age affair. We never knew who would show up on a given Saturday, but there were often as many as a dozen assorted volunteers.

I especially wanted to engage the students at this school because most of them were ethnic native Mexicans who came from small, poor villages where such inexpensive and durable buildings might well be appreciated.

As it turned out, despite the interest shown by some of the girls, the student volunteers were almost entirely male, which I am sure was a cultural bias for appropriate gender activity.

We dug a rubble trench foundation, and then filled the first few course of bags with gravel to keep water from wicking upward.

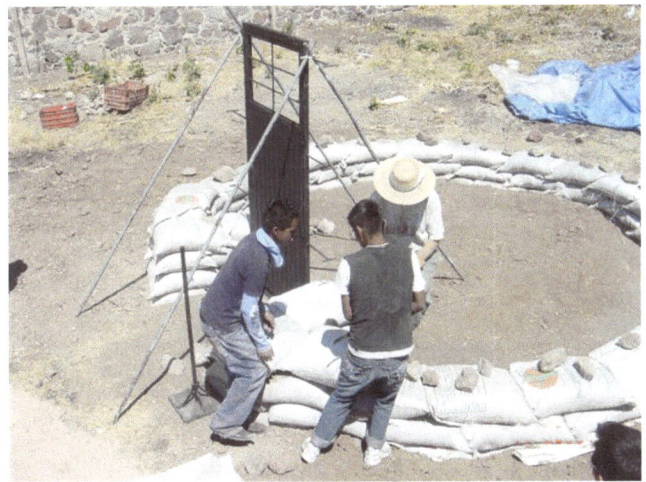

Welded steel doors are commonly used in Mexico, so I had one fabricated that had several long metal rods protruding from the sides of the frame that could be embedded in the earthbag wall as it rose.

I tried to encourage the kids to fill the bags in place, so they wouldn't have to lift the heavy bags. I even had metal sliders to make it easier to position the bags perfectly over the barbed wire. But several of the young boys liked to demonstrate their strength by filling the bags on the ground and then lifting them into place on the wall. Machismo is alive and well in Mexico!

Most of the bags were filled with a kind of road base that we had dumped there to make the job easier than trying to dig our own soil on the site. Also, I thought it would pack well enough with just a bit of moistening.

The boy in the center of the dome used a long piece of bamboo to make sure that the curvature was correct as the wall rose. Some of the kids enjoyed being up on the wall to use the special tamper we had made.

As with Riceland, we created a small loft to help stabilize the structure and use as a platform for continuing the work of building the wall. As a guide for the conical top of this dome, I set up a tripod of PVC pipe. Buckets of soil were either passed or carried up for filling the bags.

When we noticed that the perfect form of the wall seemed to be distorting a bit, I advised that we start mixing some lime with the soil before it was moistened, so that the bags would become even firmer.

I experimented with the concept of creating an arch form by simply bending some PVC pipe into an arch shape. This worked to some extent, but was not ideal.

For an exterior plaster we decided to use a cement-based stucco, which is very common in Mexico. Along with the cement, lime and sand, we added a liquid latex to make it more impervious to moisture. This was all mixed on the ground by placing the liquid in a depression in the middle of the pile, as is customary in Mexico. First we applied a rough scratch coat, then went over it with a troweled finish coat. On the inside we used a lime plaster that is more environmentally benign.

Once the final bags were placed on top of the dome, we couldn't resist assembling for a group photo.

This area of Mexico has a pronounced rainy season, so it was important to keep the dome as sealed from water as possible. So along with the moisture resistant stucco, we would put a final coating of a special roof paint that is used in Mexico for painting flat concrete roofs. This is something which would ideally be renewed every few years.

We needed to screen the sand for the plaster. Here you can see that a couple of adventurous girls actually decided to join us in the work. They had been sitting on the side for several days, and we encouraged them to join us.

In the end I think that this was a very successful project. Many people, young and old, got hands-on experience, enough to embark on their own projects in the future. I assembled some books about the basics of building with earthbags that I left with the school's library for future students to refer to. And the dome itself should remain on the campus for many years to serve as a model and a reminder of what can be done.

Not long after finishing that dome, and after we had moved back to the United States, I got a phone call from the founder of a philanthropic organization centered in Puerto Vallarta, Mexico, called "Children of the Dump." He had visited the dome while it was under construction and was impressed by earthbag technology. He had the idea that earthbags could be used to build homes, both for disadvantaged Mexican families and for Americans looking for pleasant but inexpensive living accommodations in Puerto Vallarta. We had several discussions about the possibilities and I encouraged him to pursue the design of a model earthbag home that he had in mind.

Several months later he called again requesting that I join him in Puerto Vallarta to help guide the actual building of the model home. He was willing to pay my way there and support me for several weeks of consulting on site. I felt that, considering how many homes could potentially be built based on the model, it would be worth my time to do this. So soon I was flying back to Mexico.

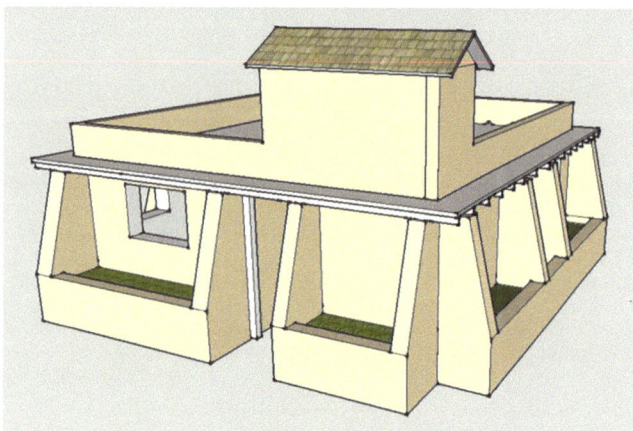

I had already done some significant design work making a digital model based on the ideas we had discussed, and this is shown above. The concept was that the original house would resemble this drawing, but there would be the potential for a second story to be added where the roof veranda shows. The buttresses helped contain some exterior planter boxes.

When I arrived the project was already well under way, with most of the walls over a yard high. They were filling the rather large bags (mostly recycled flour bags from local bakeries) with a natural adobe soil that had been dredged up from a nearby canal. The property where the model was being built was part of an equipment yard for a large crane company

and the house would eventually become the owner's personal dwelling.

The folks working on the project were a combination of volunteers from the dump recycling community and construction workers hired by the organization. I was able to give them some suggestions for minor

improvements on their methodology, but basically they were on the right track. Again, many of the men preferred to pick up the very heavy bags to set them on the wall. The women contented themselves with filling the bags with dirt.

Rather than relying on the earthbags to support the weight of the roof, the workers opted to fabricate reinforced concrete pillars at strategic places within the structure. This is the method of building that they were familiar with, and I could see no reason why it wouldn't work, and it would help buttress the structure.

For an interior plaster I convinced them to use lime; for the exterior they used a conventional cement stucco with some added colorant on the final coat.

By the time that I was ready to fly home they were almost ready to pour the concrete roof in the standard Mexican way.

Recessed Pantry

Having had the wonderful cool pantry at Peaceful Valley, we missed this facility and wanted to manifest another one as soon as we could. So as we designed an addition to the manufactured home that we had bought in Colorado after returning from Mexico, we included a recessed pantry. It would be adjacent to a large new barn/garage attached to the house, so it wouldn't be as convenient as it was at Peaceful Valley, but it would also serve several other functions.

First we had an excavator dig a hole that was about 4 feet deep and slightly bigger than the footprint of the pantry. I wanted the pantry itself to be about 6 feet underground, but I figured that I could use the sandy soil that was left at the bottom of the hole to fill the bags. This meant that I needed to dig a trench around the perimeter of the hole that would go down to the actual intended floor level for the pantry.

The next step was to start filling and laying the bags in the trench. As I did this I placed a 6 mil black plastic liner next to the outside of the bags. This would serve both as a moisture barrier for the pantry and as a convenient way to protect the bags from exposure to the sunlight when I wasn't working on the project. As the wall rose I would go around and backfill soil up against the plastic and the bags, securing the whole assembly.

These pantry walls were not actually vertical; I inclined them at a slight angle outward, so that their weight would be falling toward the embankment.

This avoided any necessity to buttress the wall on the inside. In fact, I felt so confident that these pantry walls would be secure, even with the fine sandy soil as fill, that I dispensed with using barbed wire between the courses for the most part.

I used the native sand to fill these bags because I wanted there to be direct thermal contact between the walls of the pantry and the underground soil. Theoretically, the soil 5 feet below the surface at his high altitude location would not freeze, and it would stay at a fairly constant cool temperature... just what you want in a cool pantry.

With the wall that was adjacent to the garage, I did use barbed wire, as well as long rebar stakes to help stabilize it, even with the outward incline. This was because with heavy vehicles parking right next to the wall, I realized that there could be added pressure against that wall.

Near one of the corners, low on the wall, I installed an inlet air vent for the pantry, using sections of 6 inch PVC pipe. This pipe would draw air from above ground but feed it into the space down low. The exhaust air vent would be up high in the opposite corner.

In the above photo the underground pantry walls have been completed, and you can see the huge water tank in the adjacent garage waiting to be lowered into place at the bottom of the pantry floor. Even though the tank takes up a lot of the available space it will serve several important functions.

This is a 1500 gallon tank that will collect rainwater from the roof of the barn/garage and will provide irrigation water and a reserve water supply for security. All of this water will also help stabilize the temperature in the pantry, since it will act as a huge bank of thermal mass. And the pantry will help keep the water in the tank from ever freezing.

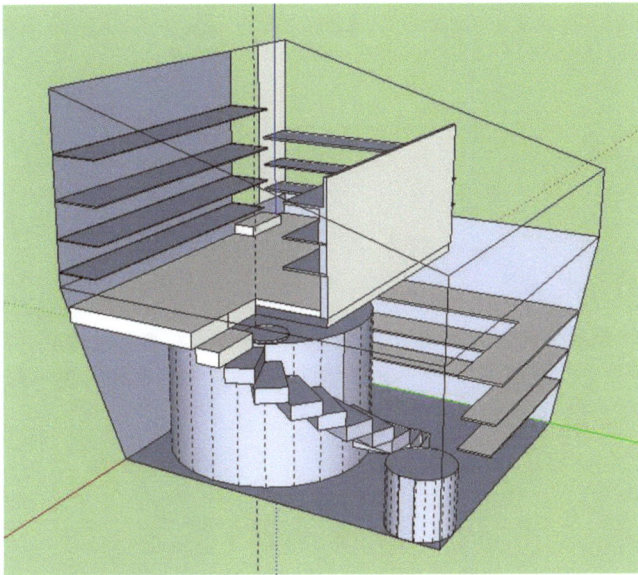

Here is a 3-D sketch I made of the plan for this pantry. The large cylinder represents the water tank, and you can see the steps spiraling down to the lower level around the tank.

Since we wanted to be able to enter the pantry at floor level from inside the barn/garage, we took advantage of this to create a smaller second floor that would serve as more storage space. But this meant that part of the pantry walls would be above ground, and those walls would need to be well insulated; bags of sand would not do the job.

I could have switched to filling the bags with scoria at this point, but for the above grade walls I decided to try my hand at cordwood masonry construction. I cut the cordwood to the same thickness as the earthbag foundation wall beneath them, about 15 inches. Cordwood walls have a cavity between the inside and outside masonry which is filled with sawdust, so this, and the wood itself, is where the insulation

comes from. Of course I also insulated the roof of the structure.

So far the concept for this cool pantry has worked well, over a couple of winters. There has been no freezing within the space, although it has come close at times. For security I installed a small electric heater on a thermostat that would turn it on if it got below about 34 degrees F. and shut it back off at a few degrees warmer. This is at about 8000 feet elevation in Colorado which has rather harsh winters.

Here you can see how the finished pantry appears, with the water catchment system from the roof of the garage/barn installed. The large turquoise pipe is designed to collect the first water off the roof that might be contaminated before it would enter the overflow to the tank. After each rainstorm, the dirty water is drained so that the system is set for the next storm. An underground overflow pipe installed on the water tank inside is directed to a sump so there is no worry about too much water going into the tank.

57

A Small Underground Dome

This earthbag project took place while Rosana and I were spending our winter away from Colorado, down in southern New Mexico. We own a few acres of desert property we bought many years ago at a county tax auction; it has never been developed beyond a small driveway carved out for parking. Basically we have just used this land for periodic camping over the years.

I have often wondered what the underground temperature would be about 6 feet below the surface in this region. Summers can be quite hot and winters are fairly mild, so digging into the ground might be a good way to develop a residence that would be pleasant all year round, with very little additional energy input. To test this theory out, I thought that somehow burying a recording thermometer deep under ground would provide useful information.

Many people have asked about burying earthbag domes, and unfortunately I know of few actual examples of doing this. So I thought that a fun and informative experiment would be to build a small earthbag dome underground on our property, place the recording thermometer inside, and completely close it up for a year.

The top couple of feet were fairly loose adobe soil that would make excellent fill for the eventual bag work. But the lower I dug, the more compact and rocky the soil became. I persisted however, by pouring water down in the trench and allowing it to penetrate the soil, making the digging easier. I was able to descend nearly five feet this way; you can barely see the handle of the shovel in the above photo.

For this experiment I outlined an 8 foot diameter circle in a suitable spot, and then drew another circle about 15 inches further out. Next I started digging out the soil between the two lines to make a trench wide enough to lay bags into. I hoped that I could continue digging this way easily enough to go perhaps 5 feet down.

I calculated that the appropriate diameter of the dome at the height represented by the top of the interior cylinder would be nearly a foot less than at the bottom, so I caved that much off the rim of the cylinder into the bottom of the trench, and started using that soil to fill the first earthbags that I laid at the very bottom.

My intention was to build the dome upwards by consuming all of that cylinder of soil eventually. In practice this concept worked quite well. It was easy

to place the bags up against the inner wall as a guide, and simply shovel soil directly into the bags from the center. To keep the soil damp so it would pack well and to make the digging easier, I occasionally placed water in a cavity of the cylinder and let it soak down.

After the bags were laid up to three courses, I felt that it was time to set the culvert into place. This required some more digging to create enough space. I set it at a position where it would support the bags that would be placed above it. Then it was just a matter of jamming the bags tightly against it as the wall increased.

After laying the first course of bags, I stretched a piece of black plastic around the outside of the bags and secured it in place with soil packed between it and the outside of the trench. But in order to be able to lay the plastic up and over the outside of the trench, I needed to slice it into several sections, as shown above. This would also allow me to expose only that portion of the bag wall that I was working on, and it would eventually provide a moisture barrier on the outside of the dome.

I needed some way to enter the dome once it was completed and I thought that a simple and effective way to make an entrance would be with a section of a large metal culvert. I found a perfect one about four feet in diameter that I salvaged for the project.

At a certain point the amount of dirt inside the dome was at the same level as the bag wall.

Each time I completed placing a course of bags, I was careful to pack soil up against it from the outside. As the wall rose, I didn't want the outward thrust of the dome walls to be able to dislodge any bags. This was especially important because I had chosen not to use barbed wire between the courses, figuring that once the entire dome were buried it couldn't expand anyway and didn't need the tensile strength of the wire to secure it.

The further I dug down inside the dome, the more of the wall was exposed, and soon there was a step

down from the level of the culvert, near the bottom.

I used the original soil dug out of the trench to berm up against the dome on the outside.

Eventually I needed to use a ladder to carry the dirt up in buckets to pour into the bags. And then pretty soon I had used all of the available interior soil and

needed to start using some that was stacked on the outside.

It was exciting to be nearing completion of the dome. I was very careful to tamp the soil (mostly with my feet) so that the entire structure was solid as it rose.

Toward the top the bags became more of a continuously spiraling pattern rather than discreet courses. The final closure created more of a mound above grade than I had hoped, but it was all quite firm.

I carefully set up the thermometer that would record the historic high and low temperature experienced inside the dome. In fact, I buried the probe about another foot deeper under the floor to have an even more accurate reading. Once that was set I proceeded to seal the culvert door with more earthbags so that I could cover the entire structure with more soil. I had to use a wheelbarrow to bring this additional soil from places nearby that wouldn't disturb the existing vegetation too much.

I realized that the top of this mound of dirt was quite vulnerable to erosion from wind and rain, so in an attempt to protect it, I collected rocks from a nearby arroyo and carefully placed them on the peak. This gave the project a distinctly decorative or sculptural look that pleased me. I suspect that anyone encountering this on our land would think that it was just playful sculpture.

If we ever decide to develop this property further, this little underground dome could be used for storage or as a root cellar. In this case the doorway and entrance would need to be fixed in such a way that it could easily be entered and kept secure.

This project demonstrates that it is possible to create a potentially habitable space with an armful of bags, a sheet of plastic, a piece of culvert and a shovel.

Earthbag Building Around the World

Nobody really knows how much earthbag building has been done around the world. The concept has only been promoted over the last few decades, and there is no registry of known construction. As the webmaster of www.earthbagbuilding.com and a contributing editor of www.naturalbuildingblog.com, I probably have my finger on the pulse of this movement as much as anybody. I have been surprised how popular it has become over such a short time; I think that it may soon eclipse strawbale building in popularity, for several reasons. For one thing, it can be accomplished just about anywhere on the globe where there is material to fill the bags with; it is not dependent on nearby forests, fields of grain, or other limited resources. And it can be done remarkably cheaply, by mainly unskilled workers.

In this chapter I will briefly profile a selection of earthbag building projects from around the world to give you an idea of the amazing diversity of styles and innovative ways that people have utilized this technology. These images were mostly taken from online sources, with permission for their use where possible. You can find out more about most of these projects at the above mentioned websites.

North America

The bag work on this complex dome home built in Joshua Tree, California for Mark Reppert was completed in about three months by a crew of five with occasional extra help. It was based on one of Nader Khalili's plans, and was given a permit by San Bernardino County. The bags were filled with 70 percent on-site soil, 22 percent gravel, and roughly 8 percent cement. The large domes got two rings of 4 point barbed wire while the others only needed one. Most of the doorways are lintels made using the tubes, but with a higher ratio of cement and also 3 thick pieces of rebar pounded through the bags. The house is buried in the ground 4 feet except for an entrance patio. They used Henry's asphalt emulsion and 6 mil plastic liner as waterproofing below grade. The cost came in at around $50,000 for just the skeleton.

I helped a friend, Baraka, design this earthbag house for the Colorado climate she lived in. She had very specific ideas about the shape and room arrangement, but wanted some input as to what was practical with earthbags and how to accomplish many details of construction. Like Peaceful Valley, the bags were filled with scoria. Often workers had their own ideas about how things should be done, and sometimes these ideas prevailed. This resulted in a few wall sections that were not completely plumb, and a few other problems. Even so, the house is basically very sound of construction and should serve her well into the future.

A 700-square-foot BLM permitting station in Bluff, Utah has walls ranging from 15 to 24 inches in thickness that create thermal mass, which produces a soundproof and energy-efficient structure. Earthbag buildings are resistant to fire, flood, and rot, making them permanent structures that are less expensive to insure. Building dirt was sand with 10 percent clay content. The exterior was sheathed with OSB board (secured by plastic fasteners inserted between the bags) and 2-inch foam. Traditional cement stucco provided the slightly irregular appearance of an old adobe building. Natural earthen plaster detailed with colors from locally harvested clay makes the inside of the building just as compatible with the environment as the outside of the structure.

The above 1,000 square foot earthbag home was built on a shoestring budget by owner/builder Alison Kennedy in Moab, Utah. It was the first permitted earthbag house in Utah. It is a post and beam structure with earthbag in-fill. The foundation was poured concrete and conventional concrete block. The bags were filled with "reject sand" delivered from a local gravel yard. A concrete block bond beam was mortared into place on top of the wall. The exterior walls were first covered with earthen plaster then two coats of lime plaster were added for additional erosion protection. Alison harvested wild clays, which she made into a paint and applied to the surface of the fresh lime plaster.

The below, left 500 square foot house was designed by the owner, John Capillo, and built in Berea, Kentucky. The code officials gave John his permit without a hassle. His design has a 16 foot dome with a larger circle coming off the dome that has a wooden roof. The lower part of the structure has thicker walls than the upper part to create some buttressing. Dense grade "lime dust" from a quarry a couple miles away was used as fill; after the lime cured it became like rock. The back side of the house was buried four feet. They used heavy 6 mil plastic barrier with a French drain surrounding the structure. For the first few weeks 7 people worked every day and after that the numbers went down to 2 or 3 people a day. This structure took about three months to complete the bag work. The cost came in around $15,000.

The dOMe hOMe in Baja California, Mexico, is based on Sacred Geometry principles, Fibonacci sequences and deep ecology. A high level of aesthetic detail was achieved by master builder /designer Rah Rysheak. Earthen plasters use nopal cactus, aloe vera and wood cellulose; this is a cement and VOC free material zone.

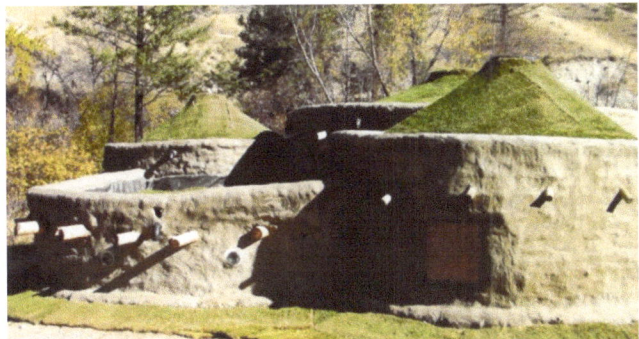

Earth Lodge 2.0 Emergency Shelter was designed by Eco Friendly Shelters in Washington State. The soil used for fill was from the excavation of the site; the wood used was salvaged from local forest fires; the earth sheltered roofs protect it from blazing sun and cold winter wind; light is from tubular skylights. It cost less than $5,000 for this 1,200 sq. ft. shelter.

This 280 sq. ft. home was mainly built by two women in Ohio for about $10,000. It has survived a gale force wind that blew a tree on it, only marring the papercrete plaster. They used crushed limestone fines (dust) to 3/4 inch in size for fill.

The "Canadian Dirtbags" built three round rooms of varying heights with two gable roofs that come together at the bedroom. They consider themselves "a couple of reformed city kids living out in the middle of nowhere in Alberta, Canada, trying to plot out a sustainable life for themselves."

This home was owner built by Martin Cubak in Idaho. The first floor is a 22 foot diameter earthbag roundhouse. Above that, he made a wood framed bedroom, and has plans to expand the house further, with more bedrooms and a greenhouse. He did all of this on his days off from work for about $5,000.

Kent Kaufman's earthbag cabin in Montana was plastered with earth, water, and straw mixed in a portable cement mixer. It was thrown on the walls, making sure rows and cracks were well filled in. He finished the entire exterior south wall in one day. He put plastic between the wall and the dirt where the cabin is set into the side of the hill.

Justin Martin's Gainesville, Florida house used an earth/lime mix for solid bags. It has an exterior adobe plaster. The thermal mass keeps things very moderate inside throughout the year. Visitors are skeptical that such a lovely house was actually built with the earth from the site. He kept a piece of interior paneling loose in order to show them the bags from the inside. It cost around $50k, roughly 1/3 or less than the cost of a similarly sized stick home.

This clinic in Mexico initiated by Cato was built on a rubble trench foundation with a typical adobe soil mix and using barbed wire between courses. It was finished with an earthen plaster. The circular reciprocal roof is very strong. It has a small kitchen and dorm room as well as the examination room. The community that it serves helped build it.

An intrepid couple in Montana spent three long months, 2,000 earthbags, 4,000 nails for closing the bags, 90 cubic yards of lava rock and 4 miles of barbed wire to complete construction of their dome home. They consumed 37 cans of Chili and had 40 pounds of combined weight-loss. They did this without any classes or courses or previous experience and with only the internet, their wits, four hands, bespectacled eyes and boundless determination.

The idea of the Half Moon cabin was to build the shell on Earthship principles but with earthbags instead of tires. The systems and design was very simple: the smallest necessary 12 volt electrical system, no internal plumbing apart from cistern-fed drinking water, all waste is composted. The Half Moon is averaging 63 degrees inside with no supplemental heating. The California site was excavated from a sloping area selected primarily because of its view of the mountains to the south.

Marcia Gibbons' Ransom Ranch project in Bisbee, Arizona, was based on concepts she learned at CalEarth. She is an artist, and made hand-painted tiles mixed in with antique collectible tiles and salvaged tiles for the kitchen. A small solar-powered system provides electricity. There are extensive vegetable gardens.

Central America

Land Trees in Panama provides courses and seminars in building with adobe, earthbag, wood logs and thatch. Their Majestic Dome served as their first structure where they learned many aspects of how to build with earthbags. Construction of this Majestic Dome started off as a small dog house but then it was converted into an "Air Shaft Tower". Eventually the Dome developed into a 2-story Main Building and an impressive 3-story Dormitory Tower with thatch roof. The Majestic Dome can accommodate up to 12 people without stepping on each others toes. This Majestic Dome used over 150 tons of earth. The exterior plaster is hydrated lime.

This house in Nicaragua was built into a hillside for the breeze, views and fewer insects. They were fortunate to have great soil to work with that compacted very well when dampened and tamped. The foundation was a rubble trench with a mixture of river rock and volcanic rock. It is an oval design of 12×14 meters or so. The bond beam and roof seemed to really bring the house together tightly. For the first layer of plaster they used cow manure, clay, wood chips and hay. The second coat was 45% clay, 45% sand and 10% cement. The final coat was 30% clay, 30% sand, 30% lime and 10% cement.

In planning to build an earthbag house in Belize, Jesse Loving decided to first build a storage shed. This building is 99.9% biodegradable. It was inexpensive to build, is durable, provides non-mechanical cooling, and is aesthetically pleasing. The building blends well into its natural environment. No concrete or petroleum-based products were used; a very small amount of fossil fuel was used to transport materials, and very little electricity was used.

La Casa de Tierra (the House of Earth) is a rental house located in Ojochal, also called Playa Tortuga (Turtle Beach), on the Southern Pacific coast in Costa Rica. The earthbags were filled with a mix of high clay content earth and sand. Earthen plaster was added to the living, breathing earth walls.

The Somos Children's Village in Guatemala has several beautiful family homes built with earthbags where families in need reside during their stay. The first two homes were designed by Guatemalan architect, Cecilia Rodriguez. They have solar heated water and grey water is recycled. The homes maintain a comfortable temperature throughout the cold nights and no heating is required. The village provides security and a hopeful future for those in need.

South America

This residence was designed by José Andrés Vallejo and built in Bogotá, Colombia in just 5 months. The design of La Casa Vergara explores the potential of seismic resistance with Superadobe as the construction technology, and contemporary design. The Superadobe uses three elements: earth/concrete, tubular bags and barbed wire. A monolithic building using this method offers the ability to create organic and flexible spaces.

Gabriel Raia Carneiro is a green builder, eco-designer, and permaculture specialist, working in Brazil. The foundation for this residence is rubble trench. Plastic was used to separate the foundation from the walls above which were filled with pure earth. This project took advantage of the possibilities that curves present in Superadobe as they express sensuality and provide strength.

Hyperadobe was developed by Fernando Pacheco of EcoOca in Brazil. Instead of solid woven polypropylene, Hyperadobe uses a knit raschel, the same netting material used in packaging fruit, and is less expensive. A concrete foundation was poured and layers of Hyperadobe began with soil that is generally about 70% sand and 30% clay, with good moisture content. The raschel is left "roughcast" to receive natural plaster. With vertical walls there is no need for barbed wire between the layers because with the open netting the soil of the bottom layer is merged with the new layer above.

This house in Patagonia was built by Paul and Konomi Coleman and is made of earthbags filled with earth. It features a double wall system that includes pumice. 500 tons of earth was moved by hand. The warm earth beneath the house, and the surrounding turf walls moderate the interior temperature. The wall for the second floor is made with volcanic rocks which are very light with lots of holes with air which work well as insulation. The house design resembles an Icelandic turf house. The walls are covered with flowers in the summer and the cabin looks like a flowery meadow.

This Community Center in Peru was constructed by a team of volunteers of the organization Pisco Sin Fronteras. It was built on a concrete pad because of a high water table. The bag work was typical, with tamped moist adobe soil, barbed wire, and periodic vertical rebar stakes. They used three nails to close the bags. They installed wood, door and window frames as they were building the walls. A concrete bond beam was laid at the top. The plaster was a conventional cement stucco. The bamboo roof was constructed in the traditional manner, first with bamboo beams that were spaced 50 cm apart then covered with flattened bamboo and a layer of plastic. On the top, they poured a layer of seashells and cement.

In the South Wing Park in Brasilia, there is a joint earthbag project between NGO Ipoema and the Federal Government. They are about to apply the cement stucco to this sensual round wall..

This house in Cordoba, Argentina, was built in stages by Leo Torcello. Part of it is a circle of about 6m in diameter. The roof is covered with straw, which helps keep it cool inside. They installed a solar water heater. They assembled reed panels for the floor, and in the pantry they made furniture with stones and wood pallets.

This earthbag project was facilitated by AuwaEarth by invitation of the local council in Minas Gerais, Brazil to offer a prototype for an ecological and low cost solution to social housing. It was a three-month project which was received with much attention and enthusiasm from the community and council, and has been well-loved since by its occupants.

This "House of Domes" in Barichara, Colombia was built under the direction of Pedro Ramirez. It has four connected domes including a master bedroom, a large living room, a dome for children with three beds, a spacious studio, and a large kitchen with center island. There is an upper terrace with beautiful views that also collects rainwater for 2500 gallon tanks.

Europe

This project was built in Poland as a demonstration of inexpensive, sustainable building techniques. It is one of many such projects initiated by the Earth, Hands, and Houses organization founded by Paulina Wojciechowska. Under the shingled roof is a partially underground dome with a fireplace. The polypropylene bags were filled with sand that had the consistency of beach sand that was not stabilized with anything... just dampened with water and well tamped.

In three days twenty people built a two metre internal diameter earthbag, Superadobe dome with an entrance vault. This was during a workshop organized by Earth Hands and Houses. They used about 300 meters of polypropylene tubing. This was intended to be a root cellar built in Sussex, England. A clay-rich soil was used to fill the bags. After five days the project was plastered with earth/straw/clay by the plastering group.

Atulya Bingham built this earthbag roundhouse overlooking the stunning Olympos Valley on Turkey's Mediterranean coast. It's on a half acre plot of land, up a mountainside and down a bone-jarring dirt road, with no running water, no electricity and no telephone line. She used earth dug up from her property to fill the bags. With an eye for expansion, she framed an extra door and topped the house with a flat roof, affording her the possibility of a second story. The house has been covered with a lime plaster. Bingham has chosen a life that causes as little impact to our planet as possible, trying to produce what she consumes.

Small Earth, with the assistance of the Hounslow Heath School, created this Earth Creature at the Southbank's Hayward Gallery in England. It is designed for outdoor learning. The long fabric tubes were filled with adobe soil and cement or lime.

This school, located under the flight path of one of Heathrow's runways, found an excellent way to mitigate the noise for children at play: they built a domed Superadobe structure that allows the kids to duck under when the noise is too intrusive. The domes have no doors but even so they cut the noise considerably.

Africa

A team of two architects and eight professors, under the direction of Akio Inoue of Tenri University in Japan, implemented the construction of an ecovillage by Lake Victoria, Uganda, East Africa. This ecovillage was designed to alleviate poverty and demonstrate sustainable building with earthbags. It is composed of three clusters of buildings, including a water tower at the center. Each cluster is composed of four living units, each one with a living room, two bedrooms, a kitchen, toilet, shower room, and meditation room. Each unit has a biomass latrine and a wind power generator that supplies electricity. It was plastered with a cement stucco.

Eternally Solar of South Africa has pioneered a novel approach to earthbag building. Long bags are sewn into three compartments, with the outer two being filled with adobe or sand, and the central channel either left as a void or filled with rebar and concrete for lintels or bond beams. This house features: solar water heating, integral grey water system, solar lighting system, recycled cellulose ceiling insulation and a permaculture garden irrigated with grey water.

Another unique earthbag building technology developed in South Africa consists of three elements: a framework of Eco-Beams (timber and metal beams that form the framework for the sandbag walls); specially formulated fabric bags, filled with sand and stacked between the beams; and, finally, the cladding of the beams with wire mesh and either plaster, timber or plasterboard. The completed structure is waterproof, fireproof and soundproof.

Brandon Rogers' earthbag project is located in Ghana. This is a guest house with one bedroom, a main space for the living/dining/kitchen areas and a multi-purpose room which will act as studio. The walls are 20 inches thick so they can resist the elements. Rogers and his crew cast floor slabs and began the process of filling, sewing, tamping, and hauling the polypropylene sacks into place. The bulk of the walls went up very quickly over approximately a three-week period. The exterior was plastered with a cement finish to minimize maintenance and then detailed with stone.

In Kitgum town, Uganda, Far Reaching Ministries built homes for employees, fellow laborers and staff with earthbags. Pictured is the first hut that they built, based on traditional architecture. The construction of these earthbag homes has also turned into a huge opportunity to share their faith and the earthbag technique of building as people gather to see what they did. Ultimately, they have reached out to house many orphans from the community.

The NextAid organization, with the assistance of Joe Kennedy, created a child support center outside of Johannesburg, South Africa. This center, for a group called Youth With a Vision , helps serve the millions of orphans of the HIV/AIDS crisis in Africa. They used local materials such as earth to minimize costs and make the building systems available to the local community. Pictured is the administrative office for the compound.

This project was produced and lead by Scott Howard of Earthen Hand. It was the first earthbag dome in Mali and Serves as a library for many villages in the area, The project employed several local people during construction. A two week-long workshop completed the majority of the structure. It is a catenary arc, reaching nearly 17 feet in height, and has a loft.

With the help of the NGO Aid Global, nineteen students from the Bergen School of Architecture in Norway built a school building in a Mozambique village using mostly earthbags. The building consists of an enclosed room for computers and an open room for English lessons. A reinforced concrete frame was filled in with earthbags, and glass bottles were embedded in one wall. The corrugated iron roof is supported over a wooden framework for ventilation.

The East

This versatile earthbag structure was built by Owen Geiger in Thailand. It is 8 feet in diameter inside and approximately 8 feet high. Plans could be scaled up to create 10- to 16-foot diameter domes. He estimated that the cost was about $300. The first two courses of bags were circles bonded with barbed wire. Succeeding courses start at either side of the door opening. He used old tires to form the door arch. It was covered with sheet plastic and then backfilled with soil and planted with grass.

Also in Thailand, the construction of this Om Dome was overseen by Scott Howard of Earthen Hand and Trevor Lytle. It is a spiritual temple for the Pyramid Yoga Center. It measures 27 feet outer diameter and 27 feet in height. The fill material was mainly adobe soil. The exterior plaster was cement-based stucco.

The Tenri University International Cooperation Project sent a group of students, with Akio Inoue as the project leader, to a village near Jamnagar, India. Local workers and students were also engaged in the construction. Pictured are three earthbag domes used for a library at an elementary school. These structures measure about 3 meters in diameter and 4 meters high. The domes were plastered with stucco.

A charity created this eco-village, called the Pegasus Children's Project, to accommodate 80 children, 10 staff, and a small school near Kathmandu, Nepal. Architect Nader Kahlili worked with them to build over 40 Superadobe domes. The tubing was filled with 10 parts soil to 1 part cement for added longevity. The series of earthquakes that leveled much of Nepal in the Spring of 2015 spared these domes, while most other houses in that village collapsed.

This "cave," in Koh Phangan, Thailand, artfully combines granite, wood and earth. It is divided into three rooms on three levels, topped by a loft. The earthbag walls fill gaps between large boulders and the double roof structure is elliptic in shape. The earthbags were filled with a mix of two different soils (one rich in clay and the other sandy in nature). Roughly 25 tons of dirt went into bags in order to form both exterior and interior dividing walls. They used cheap cement well casings for windows. The roof was covered with palm thatch with a life expectancy of 4-6 years.

"Ark Soaring in the Sky" is a school for orphans in Thailand designed by Kikuma Watanabe, an associate professor at Kochi University of Technology in Japan. The school was designed with two architectural components: the earthbag building and a light steel building with a bamboo and grass roof. The earthbag building is set on the ground floor and the steel building is for the upper floor. Three earthbag domes stand on the ground and help support the upper steel part.

Engineering Ministries International conducted a construction training workshop in Thailand near the Burma border for earthbag building and a thin shell latex concrete roof system called the HyPar. The building created was for the Free Burma Rangers, who needed a medical facility.

The Edge of Seven and Small World Nepal built a two-room secondary school in the village of Phuleli, Nepal, with no roads or airports within an eight-hour hike. A stone and cement foundation and floor was laid. The first two courses of earthbags were filled with small gravel. The remaining bags were filled with sifted excavated adobe soil. Cement plaster was used with chicken wire mesh lathe, later white-washed. The series of earthquakes that leveled much of Nepal in the Spring of 2015 spared this school, while most other houses in that village collapsed.

Another one of Kikuma Watanabe's designs is this community center for the Al-Jawasreh Society in Jordan. It is a public facility where educational and vocational programs are provided. It has three architectural components: Jordan's traditional stone building, modern reinforced concrete, and earthbag building which draws attention as ecological architecture. A passive solar system makes a comfortable environment inside the building.

Folks in the Gaza strip, who have been denied many building materials, have taken to building with earthbags. They have connected many structures that have a square, vertical walled base, which then tapers upward to form a domed roof. This allows the maximum use of space in a series of connected domes.

After devastating earthquakes and floods in Pakistan various projects have focused on earthbag construction, including this 20 X 12 foot structure. There is a buttress on the back wall. It was built on a rubble trench, then they filled the first two rows of bags with 6% cement and the rest sand and clay. After reaching the height of 18 inches, they reduced the amount of cement to 3%. The height of the house reaches about 9 feet. This house took 17 days to build, and they planned to build up to 500 houses.

Maggi McKerron of Chiang Dao, Thailand, has been experimenting with building roundhouses for guests using bags filled with rice hulls. These have much of the same insulating properties as strawbales, but the rice hulls do not absorb moisture, so this makes for an ideal building material for monsoon areas. Rice hulls are generally discarded and they are very difficult to burn (another plus for using them as walls). They are very cheap or even free. Another wonderful factor is that they are light; you can carry a few bags at a time. But of course they are not load bearing. In order to use them you need to make a framework that will hold up your roof, doors, windows, etc. She used mostly bamboo and some reinforced steel bars all tied together with wire for a frame.

Owen Geiger's Thai roundhouse is a classic of that form. He filled the bags with road base - the material used under roads in many parts of the world - moistened slightly and tamped solid. The roundhouse feels very strong due to the concrete bond beam, sturdy poles, small size and round shape. The roof frame was all bolted together in about 4 hours; the compression ring worked perfectly. It took less than a day to finish the thatch, using pre-made thatch panels. The exterior was plastered with stucco and the interior plaster was earthen.

Islands

The Konbit Shelter organization designed and built this house in Haiti for Monique and her two young girls. The interior diameter of the main space is 18.5 feet, with scalloped partial circles that extend to a 22.5 ft. interior diameter. They completed four courses a day, filling the tubes with cement-stabilized earth, and got to the finished height of 20 feet in nine days. Much of the labor was contributed by Haitians.

One of the first earthbag houses built in Haiti was the "Sun House" on the campus of a Catholic orphanage run by Father Marc Boisvert. They used recycled bags, local clay and sand from a nearby creek bed. River rocks and mortar were used for the the foundation, and a concrete pad was poured for the floor. They sewed the bags closed in order to use fewer bags and made heavy metal tampers. A concrete bond beam secured the top of the walls and the roof. The finish is painted stucco.

This is a Shinto Shrine in Niigata City, Japan was designed by Kikuma Watanabe. It was built in a vacant lot between two bridges where there used to be lots of houses and people, but after construction of the bridges, the town and people disappeared. Inside the shrine people are able to find themselves and remember their origin. The structure is earthbags and steel (for the roof).

Illac Diaz, founder of My Shelter Foundation, is pictured in front of one of his projects, a high school in the Philippines. An alliance of NGOs, the local government, and community groups manifested the school. The vertical walls were all built with earthbags and the vaulted roofs were ferrocement. It cost 40 percent less than conventional classrooms to build. Its unique design and earth material make it self-cooling and equally durable compared to standard classrooms. Also the structure is more typhoon resistant. This school has 10 classrooms and a library that can cater to the needs of 360 students.

This roundhouse is a family residence in the Philippines. At first two courses of gravel bags were laid over a 2 foot deep gravel trench. The excavated soil was used to fill the bags. 4-point barbed wire was laid in between every course. Both the top and the sides of the bags were carefully tamped solid. Five concrete culvert sections were used to frame the windows and some frosted glass blocks were also inserted in the wall. Bamboo from the property was used for rafters and split to be used to secure the native cogon thatch. A reinforced concrete bond beam was neatly poured. There is a stainless steel compression ring to hold up all the bamboo rafters as well as the polycarbonate dome skylight.

This is one of several eco-houses under construction at Plenitud Eco-Iniciativas in Puerto Rico.

This earthbag Women's Center in Vanuatu withstood Cyclone Pam with category 5 winds and helped local families survive. The building and the earthbag water tank made it through the storm with minimal damage, despite the widespread destruction in the region. Fortunately, some families were able to safely shelter in the women's center earthbag roundhouse as the storm passed through. This news impressed Bundaberg Bag Company enough to donate 1,000 meters of polypropylene tubing to build more earthbag structures and water tanks.

The Children of Hope School in Leogane, Haiti, under the direction of Matt Gunn, was built on a substantial rubble trench foundation and double bagged with 10% cement stabilized earth. They averaged about two rows of bags per day. A solid reinforced concrete bond beam completed the wall. The plaster was cement stucco with chicken wire embedded. The floor was tamped stabilized earth with a thin layer of colored cement as the finish. To keep the roof hurricane proof, they ran a piece of rebar above the tin roofing above every other purlin. The building inspector that came out even asked if they would do a workshop to teach more people about it.

The Future of Earthbag Building

I believe that the future of earthbag building is very bright indeed. If the way it has expanded globally over the last couple of decades is any indication, we can expect earthbag architecture to continue to flourish. In fact, from what we know about the enormous environmental, economic, and political pressures bearing down on humanity, earthbag building provides some real hope that we will be able to deal effectively with some of these challenges.

We know that earthbag structures can be extremely robust when Mother Nature unleashes her periodic fury, and with more severe weather predicted as a result of global warming, her fury could become even more fearsome. Earthbag houses have already withstood hurricanes, floods and earthquakes, so we know that, if built properly, they can provide safe havens. Another increasing threat is fire, and since most parts of earthbag houses won't burn, they should withstand this as well.

I have frequently responded to pleas for assistance after major natural disasters from folks looking for ways to rebuild communities with safe, inexpensive housing; their research has singled out earthbag building as a likely candidate. Initially, earthbag architecture was considered by many to be solely useful for temporary emergency housing. This is probably because of the similarity it has with the use of sand bags for flood control and military barricades. But now people are becoming aware that this technology offers a whole world of permanent architectural possibilities.

The other side of the equation of dealing with the adverse effects of climate change, is addressing the causes of these changes in the first place. Greenhouse gasses have been singled out as the most likely cause, and to diminish the emission of carbon dioxide means consuming less fossil fuel and conserving our natural resources. Since earthbag building generally uses unprocessed natural materials, the bulk of the what is needed to build this way does not require burning fossil fuel.

Another environmental threat is air pollution, both inside and outside the home. The natural mineral fill material generally used in earthbags is inert and does not off gas, which contributes to cleaner air. Earthen plasters can also be used; even lime plaster that emits CO_2 during its manufacture will reabsorb that gas as it cures. Earthbag architecture does not necessarily rely on wood for construction, thus conserving trees that also absorb CO_2.

Earthbag buildings have the potential to be extremely durable, as there is little used that will deteriorate over time. And at the end of their life, the fill material can usually just be returned to the earth where it came from. Obviously, from an environmental standpoint, earthbag architecture is superior to standard construction these days.

Economically, building with earthbags can be one the least costly approaches available. Certainly the materials for building walls can be dirt cheap. Beyond that, it depends on the building style, size and amenities how much it might cost. As with any building project, the amount of work the owner is willing to invest, and how good he or she might be in finding inexpensive supplies, can make a big difference in the cost. The earthbags themselves are generally available all over the world; often they can be recycled from previous uses.

Minimal housing can be created with earthbags for practically nothing. As I showed with the construction of the little underground dome, the cost for that was nothing more than the cost of the bags and a sheet of plastic. Of course the bags themselves might have been recycled and cost nothing as well. It is literally possible to take a shovel and a backpack filled with bags and plastic, and go into the wilderness and create a small domicile! On the other hand, one could construct a true mansion with earthbag architecture; it is this versatility that I love about earthbag building.

Politically, the future is hard to predict. Because of this uncertainty about where any place in the world is headed, the versatility represented by earthbag building is a virtue. And the fact that earthbag walls can protect a family from penetrating bullets would be a comfort to many. It is even possible to go completely underground and nearly disappear from view, as many survivalists dream of. So no matter what your outlook may be, earthbag architecture might have a place in your and your family's future.

Resources

Author's Websites

www.earthbagbuilding.com is the author's comprehensive site devoted to everything earthbag.
www.greenhomebuilding.com is the author's site all about sustainable architecture.
www.dreamgreenhomes.com is the author's site with some plans that could be built with earthbags. See the link for materials/earth/earthbags
www.naturalbuildingblog.com is a blog featuring lots of earthbag information, hosted by Dr. Owen Geiger with the author's occasional input.
www.earthbagstructures.com specializes in earthbag solutions for disaster-prone regions.

Books

Earthbag Building Guide by Owen Geiger, 2011, digital PDF. (Available through the author's websites)
Emergency Sandbag Shelter by Nader Khalili, 2008, Cal Earth Press.
Earthbag Building: The Tools, Tricks and Techniques by Kaki Hunter, Donald Kiffmeyer, 2004, New Society.
Building with Earth: A Guide to Flexible-Form Earthbag Construction by Paulina Wojciechowska, 2001, Chelsea Green Publishing

DVD's

Basic Earthbag Building: a Step-by-Step Guide by Owen Geiger. (Available through the author's websites)
Building with Bags: How We Made Our Experimental Earthbag/Papercrete House 1 1/2 hr., produced by Kelly Hart. (Available through the author's websites)
A Sampler of Alternative Homes: Approaching Sustainable Architecture 2 hr., produced by Kelly Hart. (Available through the author's websites)
Emergency Shelter by Cal-Earth Institute.

Workshops

www.AuwaEarth.com offers earthbag and earth construction workshops in Australia and Brazil.
www.calearth.org Nader Khalili's earthbag works.
www.earthbaghouse.com has general information, work/trade opportunities, workshops, etc.
www.earthenhand.com conducts workshops mostly in the Northwestern US, but also around the world.
www.earthhandsandhouses.org in Europe.
Espiritu y Lluvia located in Argentina conducts earthbabg workshops throughout South America.
www.guidingstarcreations.blogspot.com offers earthbag workshops mostly in Australia and Bali.
www.homegrownhideaways.org conducts regular workshops mostly in Kentucky.
www.naturalhomes.org lists worldwide workshops.
www.permastructure.com.au in Australia.
www.phanganearthworks.com in Thailand.
www.tsatsa-house.com in India and Japan.
www.ulewatitlan.com provides workshops and accommodations at Lake Atitlan, Guatemala.
www.unitedearthbuilders.com provides educational and charitable services regarding earthbag homes.

Bag Supplies Online

www.ace-bag.com new bags
www.agriculturebag.com new bags
www.allinsafety.com new bags
www.bagsupplies.ca new & misprinted bags, tubing
www.bagsupplies.com mesh bags and tubing
www.centralbagcompany.com new bags and tubing
www.chinawovenbag.com new bags and tubing
www.commercialbagsupply.com new bags
www.eclatindustries.com new bags
www.esandbags.com new bags
www.farberbag.com new bags
www.innpack.com new bags
www.jumbosack.com new bags
ww.maxkatzbag.com new bags
www.nmdirtbags.com new bags
www.nyp-corp.com new bags and tubing
www.onlinefabricstore.net new bags
www.pac-packaging.com new and misprinted bags
www.polytex.com new bags
www.rich-source.com.cn mesh bags and tubing
www.sandbagexpress.com new bags
www.suncoastpkg.com new and misprinted bags
www.superpoly.ca new and misprinted bags
www.syfilco.on.ca mesh bags and tubing
www.unitedbags.com new bags
www.wftonghui.com new bags and tubing
www.whitebag.com new and misprinted bags

www.ingramcontent.com/pod-product-compliance
Lightning Source LLC
Chambersburg PA
CBHW061055090426

42742CB00002B/47